PRAISE FOR

"In this beautifully written book, Genavieve Gilbert invites us all to walk in the steps of an Artist—not an earthly artist, but The Creator, Partner, Father, and Friend.

Surely it's one of life's great tragedies that many of us never get to fulfill our potential or even realize the great possibilities born within us, but in her book, *We Are the Maker's,* Genavieve leads us through her own walk with the Father and key passages of scripture to help us see the amazing, prophetic, and creative destiny the Father has prepared for us all.

Read this book slowly, take notes...pray often, and let The Great Artist unfold His beautiful, creative, Heaven-sent destiny for your life."

—Fergus Scarfe
GOD TV *Regional Director*

"Genavieve creates a beautiful space for her classes that helps me slow down, take deep breaths, and open my heart to the holy moments while painting. She skillfully advises on practical art-making and simultaneously asks the questions that allow me to tune into what the Spirit is saying and showing me. She is gentle, full of knowledge, and such an encourager! I can't wait to learn more from her!"

—Sarah Hernandez

"Do you believe you can really know God as the Great Creator? Gilbert pulls you into her story of hearing God as her Great Creator and unashamedly helps you discover a journey of creating with God speaking to the innermost parts of your creative soul. She takes you through the process of creating, dispelling each lie and building your unique creative process on truths right from God's heart to yours. This book will encourage and inspire your own creative pathway in beautiful new ways."

—Sara Thurman, EdD
Author of *Small Beginnings: A Journey to the Impossible*
and The Companion Prayer Journal

"The words of *We Are the Maker's* are as fluid as the brush strokes of Genavieve Gilbert's magnificent works of art. You will not be disappointed as you learn to partner with God's creative process and let your imagination realm be illuminated with God's light. You will be challenged and encouraged through every chapter as you partner with the Creator of the Universe and step into new realms of creativity and glory!"

—Stacey Harris
Ministry Development Pastor, Bethel Austin,
President of Leadership Resources

"Gilbert's book *We Are the Maker's* is the story of creativity from the view of creatively partnering with the Creator. Gilbert weaves vulnerable personal narrative into reflections on universal truths, passages from scripture, and an unshakeable conviction that, yes, you and I are also invited to step fully and bravely into our creative destinies."

—Josie Lewis
Artist, Author, Influencer

"I have not only had the privilege of reading about the revelation and truths that Genavieve has poured into these pages, but I have had the beautiful experience of learning first hand from her about creativity and how we can partner with God as co-creators. Her kindness, compassion, and joy are central to who she is, and she creates an atmosphere of freedom as she leads creatives into a deeper understanding of their identity.

I know this book will bless you as much as it did me as you discover all over again the beauty and wonder of our God."

—Renée Evans
Senior Leader, Bethel Austin

"What Genavieve so generously gives us in her book is rich fruit from a vineyard that she and Jesus have cultivated together. It outlines with clarity the creative process from Genesis to Revelation and makes clear the invitation of God to His people to take what is unseen and make it seen. This book in an invitation to learn how to do just that."

—Rhodalynn Jetton
Founder & Director, Wholehearted & Courageous

"This beautifully written book will take you on an exploration of wonder into the creativity of God. Genavieve brings the story of creation alive and invites you to realize each of us were made in the image of a masterful artist. Creativity is in your DNA.

Each chapter will inspire and awaken you to become who you were made to be, give you the tools to walk out your journey, and encourage you to jump into creating your own story with Almighty God, knowing that He is interested, even passionate, about being a part of your life.

Through each and every messy turn, He wants to make it all beautiful as you co-create with Him. How mysterious and wonderful! Let the words on these pages cause your heart to come alive as you discover the One who knows everything about you."

—Elisabeth Darnell
Senior Leader, Hill Country Church, San Marcos, TX

"What a gift to experience the creative beauty that flows through Genavieve Gilbert. In moments of observation as she is painting on stage, she has depicted things so beautiful that those witnessing receive personal breakthrough. On a night doing a painting class with friends, she released peace, freedom, and adventure through the atmosphere she sets and the passion that pours though her words. Genavieve is one who has stewarded her gift in such a way others follow by doing the same, whether artist or not. Genavieve's greatest gift to the world is bringing her personal authentic beauty that changes the atmosphere everywhere she goes. Much like the ocean, one must experience her to understand the value of what she carries."

—Amy Robbins,
Founder and Counselor, Pure Life Counseling

WE ARE THE MAKER'S

WE ARE THE MAKER'S

PARTNERING WITH GOD AND RELEASING HEAVEN ON EARTH

GENAVIEVE GILBERT

Scripture marked TPT are from the Passion Translation ®. Copyright © 2017, 2018 by Passion & Fire Ministries, Inc. Used by permission. All rights reserved. ThePassionTranslation.com.

Scripture quotations marked NKJV are taken from *the New King James Version*®. Copyright © 1982 by Thomas Nelson. Used by permission. All rights reserved.

Scriptures marked AMP are taken from the AMPLIFIED® BIBLE, Copyright © 1954, 1958, 1962, 1964, 1965, 1987 by the Lockman Foundation Used by Permission. (www.Lockman.org)

ISBN Softcover: 978-1-953314-53-6

ISBN Hardcover: 978-1-953314-57-4

ISBN Ebook: 978-1-953314-54-3

Library of Congress Control Number: 2021912670

Published by:

Messenger Books
30 N. Gould Ste. R
Sheridan, WY 82801

Dedicated to Arin, Anneliese, and Elliot.

Arin, you are my rock. Your constant support and desire to see me live out my destiny has changed me for the better. I believe in myself more because of your love. Thank you for choosing me. There is no one I'd rather live the adventure of love with.

Anneliese, my daughter, you bring joy into this world like no other. You truly are a princess of Heaven. Your wild heart is pure beauty. I can't wait to see what mountains you will run on with Jesus.

Elliot, my son, your tender heart and gentle strength are such a powerful picture of Jesus. I am honored to be your mom. Your hugs and words of encouragement are powerful. I love you all the way to the moon and back!

CONTENTS

INTRODUCTION

Have you ever looked at the night sky and been overcome with the sublime nature of it all? Or have you perhaps felt that mind-blowing perspective shift when your existence suddenly seems shockingly small? Questioning the origins and source of life are both deeply personal and universal. It's profoundly human. Sadly, many exert a surprising amount of energy trying to avoid questions of the soul for fear of where the journey might take them. Maybe that's not you, and you just have an unremitting hunger for more connection with your Creator. That hunger for more is likely what drew you to pick up this book.

While the answers or satisfaction we search for may sometimes feel elusive, I believe the beauty of the creation we are currently steeped in speaks boldly and unashamedly, pointing us toward our Creator. That perpetual beauty is a steady force, quietly inviting us to look into the face of our Maker and acknowledge our identity as *His creation* gloriously made in *His image.*

Like a beautiful piece of art, this story our Creator is telling takes time to ingest. We need to take time to look at it. Let it simmer. Let the nature of His heart and His words over us expose all the muck and mire that has veiled the Truth that's all around us.

For example, roughly one hundred billion stars call the Milky Way galaxy home.[1] Our sun, which seems so massive to us, is just *one* of those tiny twinkling lights. This alone would be a mystery worthy of a lifetime of wonder, and yet, our Milky Way galaxy is not unique in its vast beauty. It is currently estimated that there are more than one hundred billion *galaxies* in the known universe! That equates to 1,000,000,000,000,000,000,000 stars in the known universe! That's more than all the grains of sand on the earth![2]

Obviously the exact number isn't possible to know, nor is it the point. It's the *abundance* of it that I want you to consider. The vastness of it all is difficult to wrap your mind around, and yet it's even more mind boggling when we shift from the macro to the micro. As huge as that celestial number is, there are even more H2O molecules in one drop of water![3] He isn't just about quantity, but quality. The amount of detail in every raindrop is unfathomably intentional, practical, balanced, and without waste.

If you want to understand an artist, you must dive into their process. This includes the materials they chose and why. I can't help but ask these questions of God. Unless your vocation is in the sciences, you likely have only a vague recollection of the periodic table from high school science class.

While charts and graphs rarely inspire me, the periodic table of the 118 known elements makes up everything we see, and that inspires wonder in my heart. As if that weren't enough, only twenty-five of those elements make up *most* living matter, and even less make up the miracle that is your physical body![4]

As an artist, I know how difficult it is to create with a limited palette. Unlike me, God doesn't get His supplies at the local art store. He created the very elements He builds with, and He's done it in spectacular manner.

Thanks to telescopes pointed at distant stars, it's now theorized that the elemental building blocks of life are born in those fiery balls of gas lighting up our night sky. As stars die and collapse on themselves, they shoot out cosmic fountains of life into the universe.[5] In theory, they are the womb of the universal eco-system that sustains the Word of the Lord that brought everything forth![6] Or another way I like to think of it, these dying stars are His local art supply store.

From the macro to the micro, life is surging in every corner of the universe. It's only natural that we would wonder about the Creator of it all. Who is this genius—the One who set the earth on its axis in perfect orbit around the sun? How could all that we see not come from an artist?

With so much abundance evident in creation, we can make assumptions about this Creator the way a painting leads to conclusions about the painter. Clearly, He is wise, benevolent, powerful, and other-than. He created the perfect home for us! Obviously, He must care deeply for His creation to do it with such precision, detail, and nuance.

Moreover, through scripture we know from the life, death, and resurrection of Jesus that we are dearly loved as individuals, not just a collective unit. He didn't just create a home, set us in it, and disappear. He gave everything, even His life, in order to win our hearts. His sacrifice was a demonstration of perfect love, showing us the Father who would do anything for His children, reverberating throughout eternity! It's as if, like the death of a star that provides the building blocks of physical life, the cross is a fountain of *spiritual* life bursting forth, containing all the elements needed for life in God![7] When the bright Morning Star died, He gave life to all.[8]

I know first hand that the fountain of life from the cross really can change you from the inside out. When I first surrendered my heart to Jesus, it was three days before my fourteenth birthday. Though I was young, I had experienced so much pain already. My heart was heavily guarded. I hadn't cried in several years because self-protection just wouldn't allow for it. God wasn't on my radar specifically, but I had been looking as long as I could remember for a safe place to let my guard down and be seen—*and that's exactly what He gave me.*

It was the summer before high school started, and I wasn't headed down a good path. My friend group had gotten into so much trouble that our weekly church youth group meetings were the only place we were allowed to see each other during those long summer months.

The church just happened to be walking distance from my house, so I went even though I wasn't really interested in God or religion. Despite my aloof teenage disposition, I remember occasionally being caught by the genuine affection the youth pastor expressed when he talked about God. Though I did my best to pretend not to care as any super-cool teenager would.

Then an unexpected invitation changed my life. A friend called and explained that her parents were giving her an ultimatum—go on the youth group summer beach retreat or to rehab. She asked me to go on the beach retreat so she wouldn't have to be alone with a "bunch of Christians." She and I weren't particularly close, so even the fact that she called *me* is very interesting to me in retrospect.

A series of quick, shockingly easy things fell into place, and I walked down to the church with a backpack and pillow that afternoon, ready to play dodge-the-Christians with my friend. What I thought was a spontaneous change of plans was a divine appointment that I believe the Lord had been waiting for. He had a heavenly alarm set in the spirit, and I had no idea! I was about to wake up to His presence and a story I had been a part of my whole life without knowing.

The first night of the retreat a man preached out of Romans 7. He talked about the struggle to do what you know is right, that even when you know what is right and want to do it, you can still find yourself powerless to do it. I deeply related to this even as a thirteen-year-old. I didn't want to be making poor choices, getting in trouble, hurting people around me, *but I never really felt like I had a choice.* As I sat listening, my heart was pounding, and my palms were sweating. I felt as if he was preaching straight to me.

"If your heart is pounding and your palms are sweating, that's the Holy Spirit!" the preacher proclaimed, mysteriously reading my mind. While I can't recall the exact words, the message my heart received was, *"The God of the universe is trying to get your attention right now, and you need to respond! He gave you a conscience to know when something's wrong. If you keep ignoring Him, that conscience will callous over, and you won't know what's wrong or right anymore!"*

This thought *terrified* me. The fire and brimstone approach is not my favorite, but that night it was landing. I knew I needed help in knowing right from wrong, and the power to choose what was right. I was painfully aware of my inability to speak up for myself when I heard a "NO!" screaming inside me. So much of the pain I had already experienced up to that point was because I didn't know who to trust, who to let myself be seen by, or how to say "NO!" when I needed to.

The preacher encouraged those who were hearing God to stand up, go to the back, and pray with an adult. I didn't have much experience with this sort of thing, but several kids around me were standing with tears streaming down their faces. Before I knew what I was doing, I was standing, too. Wide-eyed. Shallow breathing. Just the act of standing was huge for my jaded teenage heart!

Shockingly, I walked to the back of the room. I was feeling intense, internal pressure to try and understand the physical and emotional response I was having to this unseen force that was causing me to act so uncharacteristically. Vulnerability was a liability I'd been trying to mitigate my whole life. This moment in my story is powerful for so many reasons, but I know God was particularly proud of me for wading into those terrifying waters of vulnerability, even if it still felt like sleep-walking on some level.

To my relief, all the adults lined up in the back of the room had teenagers praying with them already. I gleefully concluded I must be off the hook!

I did what the preacher said. I stood up and looked for someone to pray with. Not my fault they were under-prepared for the response, I thought.

I was happy I wasn't alone in my response, but also happy I didn't have to try and share such an intensely personal experience with a complete stranger. I slipped past the adults stationed at the meeting room doors and through the back of the hotel onto the beach to get some air and calm down...*or so I thought.*

The beach at night was one of my favorite spots growing up. I loved the sound of the waves, the stars, and best of all—no hot sweltering sun. I thought this was the perfect spot to breath, relax, and let those unwanted emotions I'd been surprised by subside. As I stared at the black ocean, I tried to match my breath with the sound of the loud crashing waves coming in and out, but the feelings of unease weren't going away. I looked up at the stars. It was as if the beauty of that night sky was somehow dismantling the wall around my heart.

The words fell out of my mouth before I knew what I was saying, *"If you're real and you hear me, will you give me a sign?"*

At that *exact* moment, a shooting star shot across the sky, lighting up the dark expanse and igniting a fire in my heart! Faith exploded inside me, taking aim at my fortress of self-protection. It was as if a dam broke, and waters held back for years rushed out of me. Tears poured from my eyes like a faucet.

Then I felt this gentle presence with me—like when you have your eyes closed, but you can still tell someone is in the room. This *presence* was sitting next to me, and it was as if someone put their arm around me or covered me with a warm blanket. I felt surrounded.

Suddenly, I felt things I hadn't experienced in a long time. I felt safe and covered. I was wanted exactly as I was.

I began to talk to this presence as if it were a person sitting next to me. I knew God had just responded to me, and I instinctively unveiled my heart to Him as best I could. At times, I simply wept without words, and my quiet tears spoke volumes.

I tried to tell Him I was sorry for not knowing He was always there, but I had such a clear sense that *there was no shame in that moment.* He was not pointing a finger. He wasn't waiting for an apology or an explanation. He was just delighted to be with me and to be seen by me. I didn't see anything with my eyes except that shooting star, but internally everything was suddenly different, somehow illuminated. It was like a million knots inside me had all just come undone. Everything felt new, but at the same time like I was returning to something old and familiar.

I don't know how long I sat there, but when I finally peeled myself off the sand and returned to the hotel where we had gathered earlier, the meeting room was empty. The fear of getting in trouble for wandering the beach at night suddenly gripped my thirteen-year-old heart.

The irony of potentially getting in trouble at a church retreat for having a conversation with God was not lost on me. I knew that presence was still with me, and no one could take that from me. I was going to be okay. Punishment couldn't diminish this love. I wasn't scared anymore.

I got back to my room just before they did bed-checks. My friend who'd invited me wasn't making eye contact. She knew something was up, and I didn't have words to try and explain what had happened. I laid on the stiff hotel bed that night, staring at the ceiling and feeling like I could float. The air was buzzing, and my mind was uncharacteristically quiet.

God spoke to me, I ruminated.

The idea of conversing with the Creator of the star I had seen shooting across the sky kept turning over and over in my mind. I couldn't explain it...but I also didn't feel the need to. I just wanted *more* of that presence.

From my first encounter with Him, it's always been about wonder. God loves to blow our minds, and undo us in His presence! Wonder is the posture of a child and how we are meant to live. We are invited to abide with Him in a place of childlike wonder and awe.

What I hope to do in this book is ignite—or *reignite*—your wonder, to stoke the fire in your heart, and to point you to Your Creator, who is also the lover of your soul. He's not just the Creator or sustainer of everything, He is *in love* with you. Through the lens of His creative process, I hope to deliver a deeper understanding of the Creator's heart and His standing invitation for you to run with Him until His return.

As we begin this journey of wonder together, I pray the Holy Spirit gives you language to wrap around your heart's deepest and perhaps unuttered questions.

Questions such as:

- What would your life look like if you were free from everything that hinders love?
- What would it be like to follow His lead and live from your wildly beautiful heart?
- What if you were made for more than you're currently experiencing in life?
- What if you could partner with God's creative process in every area of your life?

I can't prove anything to you explicitly, nor is it my desire to convince you to say yes to His invitation(s)—*though I hope you will*. It is my desire, however, to put on display this beautiful man, Jesus, who has won my heart. He has faithfully revealed Himself to us through scripture and creation, and I believe He wants to reveal Himself to your heart more and more every day!

I am in love with Him. Not because I've seen Him with my physical eyes, but because of who He has revealed Himself to be throughout the journey I started that night on the beach. Thank you for allowing me to walk with you as I share what the Master Artist has revealed to me from His heart. Dear brave reader, let's embrace the wonder!

I pray as you make your way through this book that the stars would align in your life, so to speak, and that every veiled attempt the Creator has made to win you would come into unquestionable focus. I pray His whispers inviting you to jump into the unknown with Him would become irresistible and that your beautifully wild heart would come fully alive in Him!

---

1. There is a lot of very rough estimating on this due to the debate on what exactly constitutes the universe and our current limited view of said universe. Some astronomers estimate the number upwards of 10 trillion. https://www.space.com/26078-how-many-stars-are-there.html

2. Krulwich, Robert. "Which Is Greater, the Number of Sand Grains on Earth or Stars in the Sky?" NPR. NPR, September 17, 2012. https://www.npr.org/sections/krulwich/2012/09/17/161096233/which-is-greater-the-number-of-sand-grains-on-earth-or-stars-in-the-sky.

3. Anne Marie Helmenstine, Ph.D. "How Many Molecules Are in a Drop of Water?" ThoughtCo. ThoughtCo, August 28, 2019. https://www.thoughtco.com/atoms-in-a-drop-of-water-609425.

4. Almost 99% of the mass of the human body is made up of six elements: oxygen, carbon, hydrogen, nitrogen, calcium, and phosphorus. Only about 0.85% is composed of another five elements: potassium, sulfur, sodium, chlorine, and magnesium. All 11 are necessary for life.

5. "Background: Dispersion of Elements." NASA. NASA. Accessed November 9, 2021. https://imagine.gsfc.nasa.gov/educators/lessons/xray_spectra/background-elements.html.

6. It's not just the stars that cause us to wonder. 100 trillion cells make up the average adult body. 8.7 million different species of animals, and 391,000 species of plants call earth home! The variation is mind boggling. Further more, 97% of your body is made of just 4 elements!

7. "Everything we could ever need for life and complete devotion to God has already been deposited in us by his divine power. *For all this was lavished upon us through*

the rich experience of knowing him who has called us by name and invited us to come to him through a glorious manifestation of his goodness" 2 Peter 1:3 TPT

8. "I, Jesus, sent my angel to you to give you this testimony to share with the congregations. I am the bright Morning Star, both David's *spiritual* root and his descendant." Revelation 22:16 TPT

PART I

UNDERSTANDING THE CREATOR'S PROCESS

CHAPTER 1

IN THE BEGINNING: THE 5 STAGE CREATIVE PROCESS IN GENESIS

"When God created the heavens and the earth, the earth was completely formless and empty, with nothing but darkness draped over the deep. God's spirit hovered over the waters. And then God announced, "Let there be light," and light burst forth. And God saw the light as pleasing and beautiful; he used the light to dispel the darkness. God called the light "Day," and the darkness "Night." And so evening gave way to morning—the first day."

— GENESIS 1:1-5, TPT

E very year on my children's birthdays, we take time to tell them the story of the day they were born. They often want to spend at least an hour looking at pictures from the labor, the hospital, and the first day of their life outside my womb. It has become one of my favorite traditions as a family. It is time consuming and often requires a shift in the bustle of normal birthday celebrations, but every year I can count on them asking me at some point to tell them the story again.

The first time my daughter asked to see photos of her birth there was a twinge of pain in my heart. She and her brother both had similar birth stories: I labored for over twenty-four hours without medication in a birthing center, hoping for a natural peaceful water birth. Both labors progressed to 9 cm dilation and then stalled out, resulting in a trip to the hospital with the hope of getting pain medication to relax my body enough to enter into final transition and then pushing. Both pregnancies ended in c-sections as my cervix swelled, and the clock ran out after my waters broke.

My daughter asked to see the very first photo of herself after she came out. Honestly, I was nervous to show her because it was in an operating room—bloody, surgical, and intense—and not what I had hoped for.

Despite my fear of how it would affect her, and me, I felt led to find the photo and show her. After searching through thousands of photos... *Did I document every second of her first four years? Apparently so.* I found the one. It was a captured moment of her tiny body covered in blood and birthing fluid with her arms outstretched to the heavens. I've always told her it looked like she came out praising Jesus. The doctor held her above the operating table where I was strapped down, unable to move anything below my neck. Every time I see that photo the same visceral urge I felt to hold her in that moment washes over me.

When I showed it to her, she stared in silence for a while. I felt the invitation to just sit and let her respond in her own way without my interpretation of the photo. Tears slowly gathered in the corners of my eyes. After what felt like minutes of silence, she looked up at me. Cautiously and innocently she asked, "Why is it so bloody?"

The first tear fell from my eyes, and then the second, third, and fourth immediately after. I was taken aback by the sudden rush of emotion. I'd been holding that moment in my heart since the day she was born. That moment happened to us both. She came into the world, and I became a mom. All at once we both entered into a new season *together*. It was glorious, but it was also scary, confusing, and not what I had expected. I consider it our first shared moment outside the womb.

Now here she was, wide-eyed and able to communicate verbally with me in her four-year-old way. I knew I was being given the opportunity to shape her understanding of that sacred moment when she was born.

"Why was it so bloody?" I repeated to her. "Well…because really important things come at a cost, and *you* are really important." The answer surprised me as it came out, and somehow satisfied some lingering questions in my own heart about that day.

She then asked about the part of the photo that showed my belly being held open by a spreader. I had never noticed that part of the photo before. I lifted my shirt and showed her my c-section scar, and she placed her tiny hand on it, as wide as the scar, looked me in the eye and said, "Thank you." Her words pierced deep into my heart, and I began to cry, again. They were tears of joy and thankfulness this time.

The stories of beginnings are important in our lives. They provide framework and context. I know I will be telling my children the story of their beginning for years to come. Every time I tell it, there seems to be a different facet that is highlighted—something new God highlights. Stories are all we have when it comes to remembering milestones and passing them on to our children. Stories are sacred. They aren't just a way of passing on information. They pass on culture, connection, and an anchor into our present moment and future, no matter how many times we hear them. Stories tell us who we are.

Why do children want to hear the story of their beginning so many times? I've often pondered their innate curiosity on the topic. No one told them it's important, or persuaded them to sit still and pay attention. Yet, they are engrossed. There aren't many things on the earth that can accomplish this feat.

I think they like to hear the story because it's a place of connection. They don't just get information about the place, date, time, and circumstances of their birth; they have a birth certificate for that. Instinctively, they lock eyes with me. They see the glint in my eye.

They hear the inflection in my tone and see me smile with tenderness as I recall the vivid details. They see and feel the love I have for them —the love that was waiting for them when they came into the world and took their first breaths. They experience the love that wrapped them up and gave them a name, a home, and a promise of a future. They feel that love when they hear their birth story.

When I read the first chapters in Genesis, I aim to possess that kind of child-like wonder. I imagine myself having climbed up on Papa's lap to ask Him to tell me again—tell me about the day humanity started.

While there might not be a physical lap to snuggle, by His Spirit, we can read the story with Him and know His heart. I don't just want the information—I want to see the glint in His eye, the inflection of tone. If we want to have an authentic *relationship* with God, it has to surpass an exchange of knowledge. It needs to be an *exchange of heart*.

An exchange of heart isn't just a nice idea—it's an invitation waiting for us that originated in the Creator's heart. One of my favorite passages of scripture is in 1 Corinthians 2. Paul writes about the mysteries of God that are revealed to us by His Spirit. Verse 10 says:

> *"but God now unveils these profound realities to us by the Spirit. Yes, he has revealed to us his inmost heart and deepest mysteries through the Holy Spirit who constantly explores all things."*

If we have ears to hear, there is so much more to glean from the first few chapters of Genesis than just information. *His innermost heart and deepest mysteries are waiting for us!*

This invitation from the Creator's heart is unique among the world's religions. Many of the stories that attempt to tell of the earth's creation have similar themes that seek to answer the question of our origin, but the Judeo-Christian story told in Genesis is an intimate account that speaks not just to the "how" of creation, but the "why." The significance, intrinsic value, and fundamental calling of humanity can be found in the lines of this beautiful story. Moreover, it doesn't tell us *just* about ourselves—it tells about our Creator. *That's* where the true treasure lies. The real beauty is in knowing *His* heart as the Master Artist.

My question to you at the beginning of this journey with the Creator is this: Do you agree with Him? Have you considered His declaration over you from the very beginning that you are made in His image? Have you settled the matter in your heart? Do you still think of yourself as a sinner, less than, or someone earning your way through life? If we believe that He made us with such glorious initial intent, we must also ask, *Why?* And furthermore, *How do I respond to such an extravagant gift?*

I believe the answer is not found in a moment or in an altar call but in a *life lived with Him,* choice by choice. In this life you will always be in process. His process. The better we know His ways, the better we can understand Him, recognize His presence and invitations, and run with Him.

He promises us that if we seek Him, we will find Him![1] You will discover unique, intimate ways in which He communicates with you directly—places where your heart and His overlap. That unique language of connection between your heart and His is a treasure worth seeking after your whole life and into eternity. I can't give you insight into that part of your journey, but I can share the parts of His heart He has already revealed to you through His creative process recorded for us all in Genesis.

THE CREATOR'S PROCESS IN GENESIS

No one is exempt from creative process. When you think about it, it's the nature of life from beginning to end and an essential part of the human experience in between. This isn't just for those who consider themselves artists. Everyone is creative because we were *all* created in the image of *The* Creator. Doctors, bankers, care-givers, politicians, and so on are *all* creative whether they acknowledge it or not.

Creativity is a way of being, regardless of vocation. It's your identity—who you are at your core.

When you begin to believe that you are creative, it doesn't mean you'll have new hobbies or side hustles (although you might pick up a couple along the way), but it will affect the way you see everything. It's empowering to know that at your core you are a maker, just like your Father. You are wired to solve problems, think differently, do hard things, and steward the earth.

The Creator made us to be in relationship with Him and to be like Him. He intends for us to function as co-creators with Him, contributing in our own small way to His creative process.

Not only are we all creative, but we *all* possess a creative process that is unique to our heart, a way that makes sense to you for moving ideas from the inside of you to the outside of you. If you've ever tried to put together a piece of Ikea furniture with a significant other, then you've probably experienced just how unique those creative processes can be. I like to read the instructions, lay out all the pieces, and make a plan. My husband enjoys figuring it out along the way. One method is not better than the other. In the end, it all comes together, with or without the mysterious extra hardware leftover.

Another way to think of the creative process is to consider it as the expression of the language of your heart. The more familiar you are with an artist, the more fluent you become in their heart language. Art historians that have specialized in a particular artist's work can easily spot a fake—not just because they've memorized the details of a painting which can be duplicated, but because they've become familiar on some level with the heart of the artist.

I want to be so fluent in the language of God's heart that I can recognize His fingerprints in His creation and partner with Him in everything I do. Understanding His creative process is a pathway to understanding His heart. It's a pathway He laid out for us in the book of Genesis.

For that reason, I am so thankful for the book of Genesis—not only for the information given, but for the window provided into The Creator's heart. It is one of the most well known pieces of literature ever written. And that familiarity can cause us to read what we *think* it says rather than what it *actually* says. I wonder how many of us are just looking for the bullet points rather than the heart of the Artist. I for one have fallen into this trap many times.

For example, a while back, I was preparing to teach a class at my church titled "Creative Process and the Holy Spirit" when the Lord directed me to the book of Genesis. It may seem obvious to consider the account of *creation* given the title of the class, but at the time the connection wasn't obvious to me.

What He showed me was surprising. He is an artist, and there is a clear pattern within His process—a cycle, a flow to His creating that I had never noticed.

"What does it make you think of?" He asked me as I read. God often speaks to me in pictures. When I'm praying, I will know what to pray or what He is saying by the pictures I see in my mind and what they mean to me. This time I saw a picture of me at my easel in front of a blank canvas. That space and how I operate in it is so familiar to me that I instantly understood several different things in comparing the text of Genesis to my personal experience of creating.

The first similarity that stood out to me is that standing in front of the blank canvas reminds me of the Holy Spirit hovering over the waters of the earth that was formless and void.

> "When God created the heavens and the earth, the earth was completely formless and empty, with nothing but darkness draped over the deep. God's Spirit hovered over the face of the waters."

> — Genesis 1:1-2, TPT

This is the "brooding" or "incubation" stage that we will explore more in Chapter 2. It's my favorite stage for lots of reasons. It feels like home, that comfortable, sweet place of resting and letting things simmer. Quiet. Focused. Turning over ideas. It's the land of wonder and "what if," and I spend a lot of time there.

God loves to dream with us, to consider possibilities, to have long conversations and explore new trails of thought. It's one of my favorite things about Him. But He doesn't just dream. After the Holy Spirit hovers for an unspecified amount of time, He speaks. When He speaks, whether He's creating the universe or whispering to your heart, it's always an invitation into something.

His words create things, pathways, and possibilities. The words, "*Let there be light,*" contain the power to create light. Likewise, when He whispers to your heart, His words contain the power to bring something forth, but He desires your participation. That desire is an invitation.

Recognizing those invitations is the heart of stage 2 of the Creative Process, which is fully unpacked in Chapter 3. This is the wonderful reality that when God speaks, we get to choose to turn toward His voice and respond. It's the moment between "let there be light" and "light burst forth."[2]

Once He speaks, it comes forth, and the execution stage has begun. This is when the unseen thing is *seen*. Light fills a once dark void. Paint covers a once blank canvas. Words begin to fill the once blank pages. Something that wasn't, now is. This is the birthing stage.

Everyone has a different predisposition when it comes to the stages of creative process. Execution is often the stage we most easily recognize in others, and if we aren't careful, we can incorrectly assume that the execution is the beginning. However, in reality, the thing being birthed has long been forming in secret. When the first ray of light burst forth into the universe, it was overflowing from its origin in the depths of the Father's heart.

The next thing to jump out at me from the creation story in Genesis was how God took time at the end of each day to evaluate and bless His work. He looked at it, while it was still in process, and called it good. *How like Jesus is that?*

After the first day of creation, when He knew there was so much more to come, He called it good. It reminds me of when I first encountered Jesus on the beach. He knew there was so much more coming for me—healing, growth, transformation—but He called me lovely.

I know from teaching art to children and adults that the tendency to be overly critical toward ourselves and our art is a learned skill. At the end of each of my art classes, I ask my students to say out loud something they like about their work or something they are proud of themselves for.

The children usually have no problem jumping into this final class activity. The adults, however, squirm and struggle to find honest words in agreement with God's heart for them and their work. Knowing this common struggle of the human heart during the creative process, I asked God why that detail of His blessing each day was included in the text.

"Evaluation plus blessing equals momentum" is what I heard. A divine equation if ever I've heard one, and I had no idea what He meant.

We will jump further into that stage of the process and its implications for our life later in Chapter 5, but for now I'll just say that if you only remember one part of God's creative process from Genesis, let it be this one: *The perfect eternal Creator God, who doesn't make mistakes, chose to evaluate and bless the works of His hands along each step of the process.*

Why did God do so? Because it was good, of course! He only makes good things! It wasn't because He needed encouragement, and He wasn't flattering Himself. I'd propose that He was showing us a secret key to His creation and how it functions.

Creation was brought forth by the Word, and it is sustained by His Word. God was imparting *momentum* to His creation.

> *"The Son is the dazzling radiance of God's splendor, the exact expression of God's true nature—his mirror image! He holds the universe[g] together and expands it by the mighty power of his spoken word. He accomplished for us the complete cleansing of sins, and then took his seat on the highest throne at the right hand of the majestic One."*

— HEBREWS 1:3, TPT

As stewards of the earth and believers who possess the mind of Christ, we likewise have the potential to speak life and momentum into our lives and the lives of those around us. We have the ability, like Him, to evaluate, bless, and nurture life.

If we get this part right, we can learn to incubate new things/life with more consistency and longevity. In a way, our ability to evaluate and bless determines the pace at which we are able to run with Jesus because that's where momentum is created. When our evaluations are in line with His and filled with truth, we will joyfully return to the hard work of creating. When our evaluations are harsh or critical, we will stall out in the desert of perfectionism or fear of failure.

Momentum is what keeps us moving forward through the cycles of creative process over and over again. This repetition then grows us to better recognize invitations and run with Jesus with more sensitivity and accuracy. That repetition is less likely to occur if we are killing our momentum during the evaluation stage with harsh criticism or false humility.

THE PAUSE

Take a moment to read through the first chapter of Genesis, and you'll notice that after each day of creating there is an intentional pause in the text, a simple pattern indicating there was some demarcation in time.

While the whole of the work was still in process, God chose to take short rests in between the days and then a full day when He was done. Again, I can't help but wonder, *Why would He rest? He's God. Why the process?*

Surely, He could have just plowed through and gotten it over with. With one proverbial snap of the fingers, and it could have all come together instantaneously. Once again, I think He is showing us a key to how His creation works best, and that's within the context *of a process that involves rest.* In both creation and in our lives, God releases power through process, and that process includes a rhythm of work and rest.

GOD'S HEART UNFOLDS

I became even more convinced of God's desire to communicate His heart to us as I read Genesis Chapter 2. In Chapter 1, He gives us a sweeping, albeit brief in light of the topic, overview of His process from start to finish. And then in Chapter 2, He moves into recapping His favorite part with more detail—*the creation of man and woman.*

When I'm describing one of my paintings, I might briefly tell you the steps that I took to achieve a certain dynamic, but I will *linger* on the details that stood out to me and made it special to my heart. Those are the unexpected moments on the canvas that, in my estimation, hold the essence of the work.

That's what we are to Him—the pinnacle of His creation. His crescendo. Let's take a minute to listen to our doting Father and let Him retell the story to us from His heart.

IMAGINE WITH ME...

Beloved, I want you to imagine with me the first moments of humanity's existence. Read through Genesis chapter 2 if you need a refresher. The Master Artist had been expressing His heart with unfathomable precision, beauty, and harmony. He fashioned a home teaming with life from the smallest vibrating particles to the largest glistening galaxies. Everything existed in perfect harmony; even the earth watered itself before there was man to till the earth![3]

By all estimations it was *already* a masterpiece, but something was missing. Something had not yet been *fully* expressed to His satisfaction. It was good, but not yet *very good*.[4]

Then everything culminated in the creation of His greatest masterpiece. He knew He was about to create image bearers to house His Spirit forever and yet. It wasn't fine jewels, starlight, or some heavenly substance[5] that He chose as His medium. No. God gathered *the dust*. Not even soil. Dust.

He saw something beautiful where no one else would. From the very beginning, even by the material He chose to create us with, God was declaring over us His heart towards us as a Father—who sees beauty in our ashes.

Before the beautiful glory, there was just a pile of dust. *Talk about creativity—He transformed dust into a human.* What a mystery that must have been to behold! What did the angels and heavenly witnesses see? Have you ever been enraptured watching someone create something? I like to imagine the angels wondering what He'd do next. Did the angels hold their breath as Yahweh leaned in close to His creation and breathed *His* breath into it?

In *The Image Maker*, Brian & Candice Simmons describe this moment, "When God breathed into Adam's nostrils, it was a euphemistic way of saying that God kissed Adam."[6] That was the moment our value was first declared—with the tender, holy kiss of Yahweh, our Father.

The body may have only been formed from dust, but it now housed the life breath of Yahweh! A jar of clay filled with glory![7]

You may not have been physically present in that moment, but the potential for your existence was, so it's part of *your* story.

I encourage you to take some time right now to imagine it. Let the images become more and more vivid as you ponder that moment. Consider these questions:

- What did the air taste like?
- What were the sounds of life around him?
- What were the smells?
- What did Adam see when he first awoke to the breath of God filling his lungs?
- Were the kind eyes of His Father beaming with delight?

This moment is the very foundation of our human existence. The manner in which humanity was brought forth and the words spoken over us are filled with revelation. It's the story of your essence—*your true self.*

> *"So God created man and woman and shaped them with his image inside them. In his own beautiful image, he created his masterpiece. Yes, male and female he created them."*
>
> — GENESIS 1:27, TPT

Beloved, *you* are the masterpiece of God. What a thought!

Just as the original mandate for humanity still stands, so too *the blessing of the Father still reverberates over your life*—He calls you *very good*. Again, don't get lost in thinking this declaration was for Adam only or just humans in general. Insert *yourself* into the story. His thoughts toward humanity were never impersonal; that would not be in line with who the God of the Bible reveals Himself to be. His blessing of humanity in that Genesis moment somehow penetrates to the core of every person's story who will ever live. These are the very words of life that connect us all as a family under one Father:

> *"God surveyed all he had made and said, "I love it!" For it pleased him greatly. Evening gave way to morning—day six."*
>
> — GENESIS 1:31, TPT

We are loved. He declared it from the very beginning! These words are the reason we can stand in our identity as the Beloved, no matter our circumstance or past. He's been declaring it, and He will never change His tune. He loved you so much, He gave His Son as proof.[8] He's given His spirit to live inside you, and He's writing the story of your life with you, even now.

It is obvious from the first two chapters of the Bible that God is an artist, and He loves His creation. You were created from the overflow of His heart, and His desire has always been for partnership with you. If you want to stand in the fullness of your calling as an image bearer, you must first understand the creative heart of the One whose image you carry!

You then must also go through the process of getting to know your own creative heart. If an unhindered heart in deep satisfying communion with God is your desire, then getting to know His heart is where you should start!

> *Father, as we explore the different stages of Your creative process, I pray that Your beautiful heart and perfect ways are revealed to us! Show us Your fingerprints in our story. Help us to understand what You mean when You call us Your masterpiece. Give us ears to hear Your invitations and boldness to say, "YES!" despite our self-doubts.*

Help us to comprehend Your love in greater measure and to receive it fully in the deepest places of our heart. Amen.

SUMMARY

- Stories tell us who we are. God chose to tell us how He created everything through a story.
- God's inmost heart and deepest mysteries are available to us according to 1 Corinthians 2:10. Genesis chapters 1-2 is a door to those mysteries.
- It is important to agree with God's foundational declarations over humanity in Genesis 1-2.
- You were made in the image of the Creator and given dominion over creation as a co-creator.
- Understanding God's creative process is a pathway to understanding His heart.
- The five stages of God's creative process laid out in Genesis 1-2 are: Brooding (Genesis 1:1-2), Invitation (Genesis 1:3a), Execution (Genesis 1:3b), Evaluation (Genesis 1:4a), and Rest (Genesis 1:4b, 2:1).

QUESTIONS FOR REFLECTION

1. Ask the Holy Spirit to help you process the story of your birth. Write it out with Him. Were you born into a safe loving environment? What were the circumstances that made your beginning unique? Ask Him if there are any parts of the story that you need to hear from His perspective.

2. When reading Genesis chapter 1 and 2, what parts stand out to you? What parts cause you an internal conflict? Be honest about any unbelief, and ask Him for a deeper understanding.

3. Process with the Holy Spirit your comfortability with the words "Beloved," "Image Bearer," and "Bride of Christ." Do you need Him to give you a better understanding of what these words mean? Do they feel like aspects of your identity that you have fully received?

4. As an image bearer of The Creator, in what ways do you relate to His creative process? Ask Holy Spirit to show you His perspective on your creative process.

---

1. "And without faith living within us it would be impossible to please God. For we come to God in faith knowing that he is real and that he rewards the faith of those who give all their passion and strength into seeking him." Hebrews 11:6 TPT
2. "And then God announced: "Let there be light," and light burst forth!" Genesis 1:3 TPT
3. Genesis 2:4-6
4. Genesis 1:31
5. *"The first man was from the dust of the earth; the second Man is the Lord Jehovah, from the realm of heaven."* 1 Cor. 15:37
6. Simmons, Brian & Candace. The Image Maker. Savage, Minnesota, BroadStreet Publishing Group, 2019
7. When Adam's eyes opened for the first time (and Eve somehow mysteriously present within him) without any life experience, past narrative, or outside voices putting false-identity upon him—his very first experience was being awakened by a kiss. A pure expression of perfect love and fatherly affection. Adam was a clean slate, born to a blank canvas of a world, with God Himself staring at Him! God made that mysterious wonder accessible to Adam through the simple act of opening His eyes. What other reality shifting transitions await us on the other side of simply opening our eyes?
8. John 3:16-17

CHAPTER 2

STAGE ONE: THE BROODING OR INCUBATION PERIOD

"But God now unveils these realities to us by the Spirit. Yes, he has revealed to us his inmost heart and deepest mysteries through the Holy Spirit, who constantly explores all things. After all, who can really see into a person's heart and know his hidden impulses except for that person's spirit? So it is with God. His thoughts and secrets are only fully understood by his Spirit, the Spirit of God."

— 1 Corinthians 2:10-11, TPT

Have you ever found yourself doing something in life that you never expected you would? Following Jesus can be like that sometimes. The fact that I have had the honor to build and lead a team of prophetic artists at my church for the last few years is almost comical to me at times. Before the opportunity arose, I had a lot of misconceptions about prophetic art, and the thought of painting on stage wasn't something I'd ever wanted to do. From the time I first heard about it, I have enjoyed watching prophetic painting during worship services, but the desire to do it myself just wasn't there.

After moving cross-country to help plant a church, I asked the senior leaders if they wanted painters during worship. I had never done it before, but I told them I was willing to try. To my surprise, they responded right away and asked if I could do it *that weekend!*

I'd love to say I was excited, but really, I was terrified. What had I just gotten myself into? I agonized for the days leading up to the service in which I was to paint.

My stomach was doing flips as I set up my easel on the stage. My hands were shaking. I was drowning in imposter syndrome! Who did I think I was? I wondered if they missed the part where I said I'd never done this before and if I was going to have to explain myself later. I prayed a super spiritual prayer, "Help!"

God's response was so freeing! He said that the only thing I was responsible for when I got up on the platform was *connecting with Him.* I was there to worship just like at any other church service, and everyone's opinion, *including my own,* didn't matter.

In that moment He took all the pressure off. I stepped up to my easel and suddenly felt like I was home. Creating with Him was a familiar place. It was a well-worn path for me—to create while worshiping—and I knew I had to create in that space as if no one else was in the room. Sometimes that looks like just standing there and not painting until I feel His presence. If I'm not connected, I don't paint.

To this day, when a new artist joins our team, I remind them on their first night painting in front of a packed room of worshipers that even if nothing gets on the canvas, they are successful if they connect with God. They must learn to access the secret place with God on stage and create from there. And even if they have to stop a hundred times to get their awareness off themselves and back onto Him, it's worth it. The painting isn't the point when it's worship; it's all about the connection.

I feel so proud as a leader when I see an artist on my team standing still before their easel in the midst of a loud and crazy worship set, allowing Holy Spirit to brood over them. That's where we start because that's where He starts.

Before the Creator spoke everything into existence, His Spirit hovered, or brooded, over the earth. Genesis 1:1 says that the earth was *formless* and *without shape*. It was only darkness. He chose to simply "be" before He "did."

While the dreams of our heart are beautiful and important to God, learning to simply be with Him is the bedrock of our intimacy with Him. That's what makes the brooding stage of creating with God the most important part of the process.

If we can learn to cultivate our secret place with God where we simply allow Him to brood over us, softening and refining our hearts, then the other stages will flow easily from that place. If we are determined to rush ahead and *do for Him* before we learn to *be with Him*, at best we will miss the mark in execution, or at worst we will *miss Him entirely*.

The Creator's process laid out for us in Genesis isn't a formula for anything. It's more like a window through which the hungry heart can ascertain the ways of God—where we can learn to think and process like Him. Through this window, we can find a life-giving process that we can create from...but more importantly, live from.

Whether we zoom in or out, we see His fingerprints from the smallest details in our everyday lives to the grandest scale of His story from beginning to end. In all of scripture, in our own personal creative projects, and even in the natural processes of life this fundamental first stage of brooding in the secret place is present.

GOD'S NOT AFRAID OF THE DARK

The first few lines of the Bible tell us so much about The Creator's heart. For one thing, He is not afraid of the dark—not in Genesis and not in your life or heart.

In the chaos of life, we can forget that He is with us. Sometimes we cry out for Him to come when He's already there! Just like that first time I got up to paint at church. I was so consumed by fear that I *felt* alone, but as soon as I turned my attention to Him and asked for help, there He was. He had been there the whole time.

I'm reminded of the night my five-year-old son was having trouble going to sleep so he went to his older sister, who he shared a room with, and asked if he could sleep with her. She told him he'd probably sleep better in his own bed and that he didn't need to be scared because Jesus wasn't scared.

She told him to imagine his fear was in a box and to give it to Jesus. He did, and then he said he saw Jesus hand Him a ball of light and put it in his chest. After that, he wasn't scared anymore. He got back in his bed and went to sleep.

He didn't need sound reasoning or doctrine in that moment. He needed Jesus. I didn't even hear about it until the next morning when they were discussing it over a bowl of cereal.

Why is it that children can access Jesus and His presence so easily? It's not magic, and it's not make-believe. I've seen my kids respond to God's presence and His solutions for them with real results, like sleeping in their own bed, that would have taken hours of attempted reasoning in my own strength.

I don't think they have special access or more of God's attention; I just think they believe He is with them easier than most adults do. And maybe it's that simple. Maybe we just need to believe in the thing He's already promised.[1]

I am challenged in this area of belief almost daily as a parent as I seek the Father's perspective. Similarly, as an artist, I am stretched because creating is always an act of faith. You have to believe in the thing that doesn't have form yet. You have to settle in your heart your belief that *you* can figure it out. If in the secret place you can choose to believe that you and Holy Spirit are a powerful team that can figure out any problem, then you are ready to do the thing!

Unfortunately, most of us don't take the time to settle those matters in the secret place and then try and find our confidence in the accomplishment of *doing* rather than in our *being.* The more time we spend in, and consistently return to, the secret place where we simply allow Holy Spirit to brood over us, the more convinced we become of His love and approval.

Imagine a world full of confident children of God who simply just turn their attention to Jesus whenever the darkness tried to mess with them. What if, like my son, we just put all our fears in a box and handed it over to Jesus? What exploits could be done by a people who live like that?

If we are to become a people free from fear, it starts with one simple thing: *love.* As a lover of Jesus, I have learned through experience that the secret place is where my "yes" gets worked out. You can read about Jesus, talk about Jesus, and hear about Jesus from others, but when you determine in your heart that you are going to seek Him for yourself no matter the cost, things get *real.*

The secret place is both mystical and practical in that we carry it inside and have access to it all the time, but it's also a practice that we cultivate over time. Those dynamics directly affect one another, too. The more time we spend cultivating it, the easier it is to access.

I've always thought the term "secret place" is a little misleading because for some reason it conjures up a quaint image of an English garden in my mind. In reality, it can sometimes feel like a boxing ring. The secret place is where I have wrestled with God, asked Him difficult questions that don't have easy answers, and often sat frustrated because I wanted more than I was experiencing.

Sometimes the brooding stage of our development involves exposing the darkness and the places that are still unformed in us. That process, if we stick with it, will solidify our "yes" because when we find Him in our most vulnerable places, we can't help but love Him more. If it gets messy, just keep going.

JESUS IS OUR EXAMPLE

The brooding isn't just where *we* settle our yes—it's where Jesus settled His. I like to think about Holy Spirit brooding over the unformed earth and wonder about His thoughts. Was He thinking about the things to come—the people who would come forth and the lives and the stories that would intertwine into one beautiful divine tapestry?

Is this perhaps the moment when He prepared all those good works in advance?[2] At the foundation of everything, with full knowledge of what would come in the fall and the pain and anguish of the cross—God said yes to the cross.[3] Despite the pain and disillusionment that would come, He was confident in His love that together He and those who would partner with Him could conquer anything. What a beautiful and powerful example He has given us!

God modeled this act of giving His yes at the creation of the world, but He also modeled it when He walked the earth as a man. As the perfect example to us of what it looks like to be fully human and walking in perfect union with God, Jesus intentionally and consistently chose to meet with the Father alone.

Even though, like us, He had the ability to commune with God in the secret place of His heart anytime He wanted, He sought out physical spaces and places to be *alone* with Him, too. If anyone had full access, it was Jesus. This is truly mind-bending when you think about it. It proves the point that we don't go to the secret place to get or earn anything, but rather, we go for the simple pleasure of *being* with Him, for relationship.

If I went on dates with my husband to earn something from him or out of some form of obligation, I wouldn't grow in love toward him. I'd actually be in danger of damaging my relationship with him.

If Jesus chose time alone to give God His full attention, surely we should, too. Luke 22:39 says *"Jesus left the upper room with his disciples and, as was his habit, went to the Mount of Olives, his place of secret prayer."*

It was His habit. Jesus had habits. Just let that thought linger for a moment. For it to be His habit means He practiced it enough that it became second nature.

Why did Jesus pray? I mean, sometimes He would say out loud to the Father that He was praying something just for the benefit of the others who were listening,[4] but other than that I wonder *why* He prayed. He was, and is, God. He wasn't fulfilling religious duty, trying to earn something or persuade God on something. I've often seen Christians in prayer acting as if they are reaching for something far away and trying to pull it into the room.

If this were actually the point of prayer, then Jesus wouldn't have done it. When Jesus prayed, it wasn't so much Him trying to bridge the perceived gap between Heaven and earth because obviously there was no gap for Jesus. Maybe when Jesus prayed, it was just a time for Him and His Father to simply be together.

How would that change your prayer time if you were to change your mindset from that of reaching for God to just letting Him hover? Yes He is within us, but He also rests upon us. Learning to acknowledge Him in both places is what the brooding stage is all about. It's as simple as turning our attention to what, or rather Who, is already there.

Bill Johnson says it this way in his book *Manifesto for a Normal Christian Life:*

> "God has called us into a place of tenderness, when nobody is looking, when there are no great decisions to make, when its just him and me in a hotel room, with no one to pray for, no one to preach to. When it is just two people in a room, that's where you learn. That's where you

learn His heartbeat. That's where you learn the presence. That's where you learn the voice. It's in the moments when nobody is watching, nobody is evaluating how good you're doing. When it is just you and him."[5]

Spending time alone with Him in a room seems simple enough, but just because it's simple doesn't mean it's easy. In the natural, spending one-on-one time alone with someone is how we get to know them and build intimacy. It's the same with God. The difference is that when it's God, there are no masks, no pretending to be something we aren't, and no covering the areas we think unsightly.

He sees everything, and His perfect love exposes all the places where our hearts are not yet aligned. It's intimacy in its purest and deepest form. And that level of intimacy can be scary, depending on your story.

Don't get me wrong—God's not scary. No, being in agreement with His heart is the safest place we can be. However, our learned fear of punishment and rejection that leads to layered, unconscious patterns of self-protection can make vulnerability on that level scary.

If we are to fully engage with Him in the secret place, we must be willing to allow our self-protection to be dismantled through honest dialogue with Him.

Again, Jesus shows us the way for this, too. The secret place with God can be a sweet place of glory like the Mount of Transfiguration, but it can also be a place of difficulty like the Garden of Gethsemane.

Because Jesus had a habit of secret prayer in His mundane days, when the hour of the cross was upon Him, that's where He went as His default. That's where he settled His "yes" once again. He wrestled with it. Without filtering, He authentically expressed His desire to the Father, and He was strengthened as He laid down all His self-protection.

"Then he withdrew from them a short distance to be alone. Kneeling down, he prayed, "Father, if you are willing, take this cup of agony away from me. But no matter what, your will must be mine." Jesus called for an angel of glory to strengthen him, and the angel appeared. He prayed even more passionately, like one being sacrificed, until he was in such intense agony of spirit that his sweat became drops of blood, dripping onto the ground."

— LUKE 22:4-44, TPT

We may not wrestle in the secret place to the point of sweating drops of blood as Jesus did, but we are meant to have that level of unveiled intimacy with Him, being exactly who we are in the moment and allowing God's presence to breathe life into us.

The best example I can think of for this is a baby in the womb[6] as it is floating and simply receiving life. Ironically, the thing we did *naturally* in the womb is the thing we later have to *learn* as adults. After we are born, the dynamic of simply being in God's presence while He forms us doesn't disappear—it just moves to the inside of us. The secret place of the womb transforms into the secret place of our hearts. Our hearts become the womb. Our lives are then birthed from our hearts, through our choices.

What you incubate inside you will always come out of you eventually.[7] Your mind is a secret place where no one knows what's going on except you and God. How kind is God that He's given us this buffer? He designed us in such a way that we have the ability to cultivate our life from the inside out with Him. Your thoughts and the internal space of your mind are a womb of possibilities that you carry around with you everyday. And it's not just your thoughts, but your imagination, too. Your imagination can be a powerful tool in the brooding stage if you learn to use it.

YOUR IMAGINATION IS A PORTAL

We tend to think of the imagination as just for kids. We use phrases like "that's just your imagination" to dismiss things we can't explain. "He's got a BIG imagination" implies that someone may be lying. Adult christians are conditioned to dismiss and ignore our imaginations and believe that only bad things come from it. As an adult, it's just not talked about much. I want to suggest though that our imaginations are an important part of our beings and our relationship with God.

Let me just take a moment to talk about what the imagination is, and then I'll share a story about how the imagination realm has greatly impacted my life. I like to think about the imagination as the projector screen of your mind. It's also referred to as the "mind's eye" or "eyes of your spirit."

The imagination is not good or bad in and of itself. It's neutral in the same way a television is neutral. What you project onto it determines if it's good or bad for you. Sometimes, it switches on involuntarily, and we see images in our mind without obvious provocation. Other times, we have to intentionally engage with it. In this way, it's like a muscle, and the more we exercise it, the stronger it gets.

I refer to the imagination as a *realm* because I believe Jesus gives us precedence to do so. In the Sermon on the Mount, Jesus says, *"Your ancestors have been taught, 'Never commit adultery.' However, I say to you, if you look with lust in your eyes at the body of a woman who is not your wife, you've already committed adultery in your heart."*[8] This passage teaches us that there is a dynamic to what happens inside of us that is tangible, even though it isn't seen by others.

Jesus didn't say, *When you've done it in your heart, it's almost as if you've done it for real.* No, He said that if you see it and you lustfully choose to allow it to stay and play out in your mind, it's the *same* as doing it. If this is true for the negative images, then it can be also true for the positive. In other words, we can use that same projector screen of our imagination to encounter God, have conversations with Him, and learn to be with Him!

I have experienced this first hand. When I found out I was pregnant for the second time, it was a surprise (even though I already knew it in my spirit somehow). I was playing with my daughter who was about fifteen months old at the time, and suddenly, it felt like there was a third person in the room with us.

I said out loud, "I think your brother just joined us," before I even knew what I was saying. I laughed at how ridiculous that thought was because we weren't trying to get pregnant, but then immediately I felt the Lord's smile and knew something was up. I quickly counted the days and realized I was late. Sure enough, a quick trip to the drug store confirmed I was indeed pregnant.

I quickly embraced the idea of having another baby, but I was scared of the birth since my first didn't go to plan. The thought of adding to our family somehow brought lots of deep emotions to the surface that were previously tucked away. I became conscious of a feeling I'd been experiencing in response to my infant daughter's entrance into my life.

When I looked at her face, all I saw was innocence, purity, and beauty. The Lord whispered that I possessed those things in the same measure. I knew it was true if He was saying it, but I was also aware that I didn't *feel* it. I couldn't remember the last time I felt innocent. I understood theologically I was made innocent by Jesus, but I didn't feel it, and I had a suspicion as to why.

This dissonance led me to seek out some more inner healing through a prayer ministry that focused on helping those affected by sexual trauma. For the nine months of my pregnancy with my son, I met with a small team of intercessors every other week, and we spent hours together as Jesus led me on a journey of restoring my awareness of my innocence.

During this season, He would show me these vivid images in my mind, and as I described them to the intercessors in the room, they would help me interact with Jesus and gain insight and understanding. I lost count of how many times He brought me through an unexpected series of questions and answers that brought His Truth face-to-face with the un-truth in my heart.

Even though every encounter was powerful and resulted in the fruit of a renewed mind and my spirit strengthened, I would wrestle with how much of it was "just my imagination." I just didn't understand how allowing Him to show me a picture in my mind and then having a conversation about it could possibly hold the power to undo years of trauma. The pictures and places often became so detailed and immersive that I could see, hear, and smell my surroundings in my imagination with more awareness than I had of the room I was physically sitting in.

I mention this because unbelief is a sickness of the heart often caused by pain or trauma, and it keeps us from fully receiving the things of God that are available to us as His children. Like the Pharisees who saw Jesus move in miracles but still wouldn't receive Him, I was having vivid, beautiful encounters with Him that bore fruit in my life, but unbelief would still creep in and try to keep me from fully receiving it. If you experience unbelief when you go to the secret place with Jesus, you're not alone. It doesn't mean something's wrong with you. It just means your faith is in process. Don't quit.

One of the most common places I would meet Jesus during these encounters was in a small row boat, which became a symbol of safety and intimacy. Some days in that season I would simply hear Him whisper in my spirit, "Get in the boat." I knew immediately it was an invitation to come away, and wherever I was, I had access to this safe, presence-filled space where I could just be with Him.

Sometimes we would have detailed conversations in which He unveiled things to me that I needed to hear. Other times we would just sit in silence, and I could hear the water lapping the sides of the boat and the sun warming my face. I sat in that boat with Him for so many hours, and the details became so vivid that "getting in the boat" was a well-worn path I could easily access anywhere...even in an Operating Room.

Throughout that season of inner healing we would talk a lot about the up-coming birth, and He would calm my heart by telling me about my son. But no matter how many times I asked, He never assured me I would have the pain-free VBAC[9] I was hoping for. When the contractions started, I heard Him say, "Get in the boat."

For over twenty four hours I labored in the same birthing center I had labored in with my daughter—my amazing husband and doula by my side. I progressed to 9.5 cm, just like the first time, and then stalled. The midwives tried everything they could to help my body relax and move into transition, but we made no progress. Then, during one particularly difficult contraction, I knew in my spirit I needed to get to a hospital.

With an unusual clarity and certainty, I looked at my husband and told him we needed to drive to the hospital. The midwife said she was comfortable with me laboring for another two hours, but I just knew we needed to go.

We met my OB at the hospital who was very pro-VBAC and whom I'd met with in advance to discuss my wishes for avoiding another cesarean. She was confident that some pain meds would help my body relax and finish dilating.

After an epidermal and several more hours of unfruitful contractions, my cervix began to swell, and I was losing dilation. My son's heartbeat was also struggling to recover after each contraction. My OB held my hand and broke the news to me that we needed to get the baby out. With tears streaming down my face, I pictured my son in my arms, just like Jesus had shown me, and I consented.

As they started wheeling me down the hall I heard Him again, "Get in the boat." Immediately, I was there as I became less and less conscious of my surroundings. When I got in the boat this time, I heard Jesus singing. I began to sing with Him as we held eye contact. His eyes were filled with so much strength and peace. In the natural I was strapped down to the operating table with the epidural up to my neck. I couldn't even feel myself inhaling and exhaling. By all expectations, I should have been scared or at least anxious, but I wasn't. I was in the boat with Jesus.

I felt the pressure of my son being pulled out of me and then waited to hear his cry. One Mississippi. Two Mississippi. Three Mississippi. "Is he ok?" I choked out. Three more seconds of deafening silence went by before I finally heard him cry out. "It just takes a second some-times," I remember my OB saying over the paper curtain between us.

I called out to my son, hoping my familiar voice would soothe him in the absence of my embrace. As I waited for my husband to bring our son over for me to see him, I became more aware of the physical ache to hold him and less aware of the boat. Waiting to see him and touch our cheeks together was the hardest part of the whole experience.

The desire to hold your child in that moment of newness is so deep and visceral. Finally getting to feel his soft, warm cheek against mine was like crawling across a parched desert and finally getting a cold drink. I can only imagine what it feels like to the Father when He gets to embrace a child that has been away from Him.

My husband then held my son, and I just got back in the boat to sing with Jesus again. When I am in that place with Jesus, time passes differently. It felt like maybe five minutes, but apparently forty-five minutes had passed when I heard my OB talking with my husband. He was gently swaying our son to sleep while she was explaining why it was taking so long, and why she called in her partner to help.

All I remember hearing was something about working quickly and the tremble in my husband's voice. I looked up at the anesthesiologist who was sitting right behind my head. He smiled and said he'd never heard a mom singing while giving birth.

Some time later, after settling into our room with our son my doctor came to check on us and explained what had happened. She explained that when she was opening me up, my son punched his fist through the opening, and I tore in two directions, bursting a few blood vessels. After they got him out as quickly as possible, I was literally bleeding out. For almost forty minutes, she and the other doctor worked fever-ishly to repair the blood vessels and stop the bleeding.

She said they got it just in time and were going to watch me through the night to determine if I needed a blood transfusion due to the excessive blood loss. Those two women saved my life, and I never knew I was in danger of losing it. I was in the boat.

My daughter's C-section took all of ten minutes from the time they wheeled me in to the time they were sewing me up—*but it felt like hours*. My son's C-section took an hour, but it felt like 5 minutes —*because I was with Jesus*. Being with Him in the boat didn't change the circumstance, but it definitely changed how I experienced it. That's the power of brooding in the secret place.

I tell you this story because that was when my unbelief vanished. What happened on the inside of me in my imagination had real reper-cussions in the world outside of me. My imagination was the vehicle that carried me into an encounter with Jesus while I was in the midst of a terrifying situation.

When He is present, everything changes. He is not anxious, and when our hearts are aligned with His, we aren't anxious either. If this is possible in the midst of a c-section with complications, then surely it's possible in our everyday lives.

To ignore the gift of a redeemed imagination is to forfeit potential encounters with God. It is one of the most powerful gifts God has given you, and cultivating it will greatly impact your life. Because when we encounter Him, we don't walk away the same.

Does He break in and meet us in the glorious mountain top experi-ences? Yes. There is clearly a biblical precedence for this, but He also wants to encounter us in the other 99% of life. Learning to let Him brood over us turns even the mundane tasks of life into something sacred.

In the end, it's not the things we've accomplished that we will give an account for—it's the amount of love with which we lived. In other words, *being* with Him is more vital than *doing* for Him. That brooding produces intimacy, and intimacy is what empowers us to truly run with Him.

The concept of "running with God" as described in Song of Song 2:13,[10] isn't just referring to signs, wonders, and miracles. Rather, running with God means *partnership* with Him in your everyday life. I like to think of it like a three-legged race. The process of running with God requires the same element of leaning into Him and surrendering to *His* pace because, though we are partners, He is leading. This is how we're meant to walk out our lives when we've chosen to bind ourselves to Jesus.

If we are going to walk in partnership with Jesus in this way, we must become students of His *movements* and *pace*. My husband and I love to cook together for our family. We have done it so much over the years that we are in tune with each other's movements, and when we aren't "hangry," we move in rhythm together, anticipating each other's pace. We learn the same kind of syncopation with God through everyday life with Him, but there are also some clues in scripture that tell us how He thinks and processes.

In Song of Songs He is described as a graceful gazelle and a skipping young stag.[11] Maybe that imagery is familiar to you, but I had to google a video of a gazelle and see how it moves to understand the reference.

What I found was an animal with pogo sticks for legs! It bounced around, light as a feather, like a ballerina in the *Nutcracker!* It reminded me of a butterfly moving from flower to flower, barely disturbing its landing area.

This is how He is. His burden is light, and ours is not meant to feel any heavier. If we are to partner with Him, to move in step with Him, then how do we become the butterfly version of ourselves? The cocoon—*nature's secret place.*

METAMORPHOSIS

What does the cocoon look like in our everyday lives? Prayer. In theory, prayer is a beautiful, mystical idea. In practice, it is a place of metamorphosis. I love the heart-level description of prayer that C.S. Lewis gave us when he said this:

"I pray because I can't help myself. I pray because I'm helpless. I pray because the need flows out of me all the time, waking and sleeping. It doesn't change God. It changes me."

When we think of the butterfly emerging from the cocoon, it is easy to see the product and be in awe, but not consider the process. When we consider what goes on *inside* the cocoon, before the beautiful wings take their first flight, there is a powerful metaphor to be pondered.

When caterpillars are ready to be transformed, they actually create what's called a chrysalis, which you may recall from science class. What I didn't learn in science class though is that the caterpillar's skin becomes the hard outer shell of the chrysalis as it detaches from it's own body, and its insides dissolve into caterpillar soup! Everything but a few key structures and small clusters of cells called imaginal discs dissolve and then mysteriously rearrange themselves into a completely different structure.

These imaginal discs consist of about fifty cells to begin with and then multiply to thousands just to make one wing in a matter of weeks. One might assume this is a sort of death and rebirth with no connection between the butterfly and caterpillar, but a study done in 2008 suggests otherwise. Researchers trained a group of caterpillars to have an odor aversion by giving an electric shock in association with a chemical. When the adult butterflies emerged, they still exhibited an aversion to the odor when released.[12] They remembered things from their larvae stage even though they were liquified!

A few parallels come to mind. First, you already contain everything you need to fly. Maybe you've caught a glimpse in your spirit of what it might look and feel like to partner with God in a more consistent and intimate way—to fly with Him and release His Kingdom into the earth. You already have what's needed to partner with God in boldness and freedom because you were designed for it! You must simply surrender to incubation in the cocoon. Practically, that might look like a season of saying no to other things so you can say yes to the secret place.

Second, the practice of prayer and cultivating the secret place can feel like death. It can feel like you are dissolving, losing yourself as you surrender to His ways. Laying down your will when self protection is telling you to fight for your rights can be challenging. Remember Jesus's words when you find yourself in this battle:

> "For if you choose self-sacrifice, giving up your lives for my glory, you will embark on a discovery of more and more of true life. But if you choose to keep your lives for yourselves, you will lose what you try to keep."[13]

The last thing that stood out to me was the memory the adult butterfly has from its larvae stage. The essence of who you are and the memories of your life before Jesus don't change. You just get to see them through new eyes. You get to interpret them with the mind of Christ.

When I went through the season of healing prayer that I mentioned earlier, I spent a lot of time recalling with Jesus some painful memories of trauma and pain. He didn't take the memories away, He just showed me where He was in the midst of them. He gave me a new perspective and took away the need to self-protect.

When you see someone who seems to walk in step with Jesus, releasing His Kingdom and oozing His goodness, just know there was a process that led them there. They didn't wake up that way. They have cultivated something with Him on the inside that probably felt a lot like death while it was being developed.

That leads us to the all important question: *How do we know when it's time to fly?* How do you discern if you are uncomfortable because of the incubation process or if the cocoon is getting too tight and you are ready to emerge? Once you get used to the cocoon, it's easy and enjoyable to just get lost in the depths of God's presence—*but there comes a time when God issues an invitation to exit!*

Recognizing that invitation is very important. It is so vital, in fact, that I think it deserves its own chapter. It may be the shortest stage, but it's potentially the most important to learn to recognize because it will keep you in step with His timing. It is the moment when all the hard work done in the brooding stage begins to take shape and be realized.

This next stage is the first physical manifestation in the *visible* realm of the *invisible* realities that were forming and taking root within you in the secret place. The better we become at the art of recognizing God's invitations, the more likely we are to say yes to them!

CHAPTER SUMMARY

- If we are determined to rush ahead and *do with Him* before we learn to *be with Him,* we are in danger of missing Him completely.
- God isn't afraid of the dark—not at the beginning and not in your heart.
- Jesus settled His "yes" to the cross during the brooding stage at the beginning of creation as well as in the Garden of Gethsemane.
- It's okay if the secret place doesn't come naturally. Don't give up.

- Your imagination is a powerful tool in the brooding stage.
- Faith is a process, and unbelief is rooted out in the brooding stage.
- To ignore the gift of a redeemed imagination is to forfeit potential encounters with God.
- A season of brooding might mean you have to say no to some things in order to say yes to the secret place.

IMAGINATION REALM ACTIVATION

"I pray the light of God will illuminate the eyes of your imagination, flooding you with light, until you experience the full revelation of the hope of his calling—that is, the wealth of god's glorious inheritances that he finds in us, his holy ones!"

— EPHESIANS 1:18, TPT

Encountering Jesus with your imagination, or your mind's eye, is possible for every Image Bearer. You might feel like it's a gifting you don't possess, but this isn't a gift as much as a skill. You already have the hardware; you just need to learn how to use it. I have personally used this tool in the secret place with Jesus for years, and it is so powerful.

As a simple activation to prove my point, I want you to picture a cow in your mind right now. You probably don't even have to close your eyes to do it because it has nothing to do with your eyes. Now picture that cow painting a picture. Can you see it? If this is difficult for you, take your time. The more time you focus on it, the more detail will develop. It's that simple!

Now, using that same ability to project images in your mind, you are going to picture the scene I am about to describe. The less distractions, the better, so take some time to prepare the space. Quiet instrumental music might be helpful in aiding you while you are growing in this. As you are picturing the scene in your mind, pay particular attention to what you see, hear, smell, and feel. The more senses you engage, the more immersive it will become. Also, have a journal ready to record what you see, or if that feels too distracting, you can use a recorder.

After you have settled yourself into a quiet space, I want you to imagine you are walking along the beach at sunset. The sky is filled with the most magnificent array of colors you've ever seen. The water is calm, and the gentle lapping of waves on the shore washes over your feet. The smell of salt is in the air, and you can hear seagulls in the distance. Your bare feet sink into the warm, wet sand with each step, and your breathing slows as your body relaxes.

Once you have established this image in your mind, take some time to look around and enjoy it. As your surroundings become clearer to you and you are ready, imagine Jesus walking up alongside you. You are now walking along the shore together. From here, the encounter is yours. Talk to Him like you would a best friend, and don't second guess yourself as you hear His responses. If you feel silly, talk to Him about it.

The more you do this, the easier it will get. And those personal places of encounter will become a beautiful part of your history with God.

MY PRAYER FOR YOU

Father, I pray for those who will engage with this exercise to have a hedge of protection around them. I ask You for angels to fill the room and Your glory to manifest. I pray for grace to surrender self-protection, and courage to embrace belief. Enlighten the eyes of their imagination, and fill them with revelation! Amen.

---

1. "Don't be obsessed with money but live content with what you have, for you always have God's presence. For hasn't he promised you, "I will never leave you alone, never! And I will not loosen my grip on your life!" Hebrews 13:5 TPT

2. Ephesians 2:10

3. Revelation 13:8

4. John 12:30, John 11:41 Jesus loudly prayed when He raised Lazarus from the dead not to make His prayer more powerful or likely to be heard, but for the benefit of those who were listening.

5. Johnson, Bill. *Manifesto for a Normal Christian Life.* Redding, CA: Bill Johnson Ministries, 2013.

6. For the purposes of this book, when I refer to one's "heart" I am referring to their spirit and soul together within them. This is the understanding I have from the Bible when it refers to the heart of a man. His soul is the personality and consists of the mind, will, and emotions, and the spirit is the eternal part that knows God, understands Truth, and submits to Holy Spirit's leadership.

7. *"You'll never find a choice fruit hanging on a bad, unhealthy tree. And rotten fruit doesn't hang on a good, healthy tree. Every tree will be revealed by the quality of the fruit that it produces. Figs or grapes will never be picked off thorn trees. People are known in the same way. Out of the virtue stored in their hearts, good and upright people will produce good fruit. But out of the evil hidden in their hearts, evil ones will produce what is evil. For the overflow of what has been stored in your heart will be seen by your fruit and will be heard in your words."* Luke 6:43-45 TPT

8. Matthew 5:27-28 TPT

9. Vaginal Birth After Cesarean

10. "Can you not discern this new day of destiny breaking forth around you? The early signs of my purposes and plans are bursting forth. The budding vines of new life are now blooming everywhere. The fragrance of their flowers whispers, "There is change in the air." Arise, my love, my beautiful companion, and run with me to the higher place. For now is the time to arise and come away with me." SOS 2:13 TPT

11. "But until the day springs to life and the shifting shadows of fear disappear, turn around, my lover, and ascend to the holy mountains of separation without me. Until the new day fully dawns, run on ahead like a graceful gazelle and skip like the young stag over the mountains of separation. Go on ahead to the mountain of spices—I'll come away another time.: SOS 2:17 TPT

12. Blackiston, Douglas J, Elena Silva Casey, and Martha R Weiss. "Retention of Memory through Metamorphosis: Can a Moth Remember What It Learned as a Caterpillar?" PloS one. Public Library of Science, March 5, 2008. https://www.ncbi.nlm.nih.gov/pmc/articles/PMC2248710/.

13. Luke 9:24, Matthew 16:25

CHAPTER 3

STAGE TWO: RECOGNIZING
THE INVITATION

"Can you not discern this new day of destiny breaking forth around you? The early signs of my purposes and plans are bursting forth. The budding vines of new life are now blooming everywhere. The fragrance of their flowers whispers, "There is change in the air." Arise, my love, my beautiful companion, and run with me to the higher place. For now is the time to arise and come away with me."

— SONG OF SONGS 2:13, TPT

As laid out in the previous chapter, learning to simply *be* with God is the heart of the brooding stage. And as demonstrated by Genesis 1:1, it is also the starting place for God's creative process. In God's upside-down Kingdom, He seems to do everything from the inside out, as opposed to the world's systems of performance and earning one's way.

THE INVITATION TO RUN WITH HIM

Truly, to become the resting place of God's presence should be the foundation of our relationship with Jesus, but there comes a time when that intimacy of the secret place is tested. An adventure is laid before us, and like the Shulamite of the Song of Songs, we are invited to run with Him into unknown territory.[1]

His invitations into the unknown are often subtle and always voluntary. He lets us choose because He wants voluntary lovers. In a sense, our love is put into action when we are invited into a new way of running, or relating, with Him.

It would be nice to think we will always accept His invitations, but the truth is we won't. Sometimes, we simply miss it. Other times, we are too scared of change, and we deny Him. Like the Shulamite, we love Him, but we also fear the unknown. All fear is a threat to love—it is not an idle threat.

In God's kindness He shows us through the allegory of the Song of Songs how He responds to our rejection. In perfect love, He does not seek to control us. He honors our no but never gives up on pursuing our heart. In the Shulamite's case, He goes and runs on the mountains without her while she is consumed with longing for His return.

Learning to recognize and embrace the divine invitations is the key to unlocking life-long adventures with Jesus and avoiding the stagnancy, futility, and emptiness of a religious spirit. I'll share an example from a time I experienced the tension that often accompanies an invitation to run with the Lord.

AN INVITATION TO MORE

It was November 11, 2009, and I had been living in Kansas City for over a year, attending the International House of Prayer. Something was happening that week that drew in a large Asian crowd from overseas, and I was enjoying being surrounded by fiery intercessors worshiping and praying in languages I didn't understand.

I remember having my sketchbook with me in the prayer room that afternoon, which was unusual at the time. The words of the chorus being sung from the stage were, "I want to give all that's inside of my heart to You." I drew a heart in my sketchbook that was gushing like a fountain with the words of the chorus written over it. I was very much enjoying myself and planned to camp out, right where I was, for the rest of the day, incubating in the goodness of God's presence.

I happened to look at my phone and saw a text from a friend named Genevieve. (Yes, we know how cool that is!) The text read something to the effect of, "Get down to the EGS building as soon as you can. God's Spirit is breaking out."

I thought that was awesome, but I felt God's Spirit exactly where I was, and I was super content in my prayer room nook. My phone buzzed again, "SERIOUSLY! GET DOWN HERE!" I got chills. I asked the Lord what I should do and felt Him smile, so I decided to go check it out.

I noticed as I drove into the parking lot that there were way more cars than usual for that time of day. Something was obviously going on. When I walked through the doors, the air was electric. Instantly the hairs stood up all over my body. Even now I can feel it. The sound that came from the room as I slowly entered was a chorus of laughter, singing, and joyful noises. It washed over me and pulled me forward into its current.

People were all over the place—lying on the floor, laying on chairs, dancing, singing, and being sloshed around in groups that looked like human tornados. Some were flopping on the ground, laughing uncontrollably. I had NEVER seen anything like this.

This was certainly not normal for these sober-minded people of prayer. It felt like it took me an hour to wander in towards a seat. It was so unusual that honestly, I felt scared at first. A place that had been my spiritual home for over a year suddenly felt unfamiliar, and I didn't like it.

One of the leaders of the house got on the mic and tried explaining what was happening, but he was having trouble speaking and standing. He explained bits of a story I would later come to hear many more times about the origins of this outpouring.

Evidently, during one of the ministry school classes, God encountered a young woman. He set her free from self-hatred that was left in the wake of a past trauma. As she shared with the class about her new-found freedom, others began to get set free, too. Radical joy came upon the whole group.

In an effort to not limit the obvious move of the Holy Spirit, the teachers decided to let the meeting go on as long as He was moving and setting hearts free. This turned into over nine months of extended meetings as thousands of people experienced a unique move of God. People flooded in from all over the world to enjoy this unique outpouring.

Before I experienced those nine life-changing months, I was just a lover of Jesus, scared out of my mind by the craziness before me. That first night, I watched wide-eyed as people I knew and respected flopped on the ground, laughed until they cried, and acted as if they were drunk. It was so confusing and so exposing of my heart. I honestly regretted leaving my cozy corner of the prayer room.

After I found my friend who had texted me, I began to cry. Seeing a familiar face suddenly allowed me to acknowledge how unfamiliar all this felt. She stood with me, steady as can be, and told me to ask Holy Spirit what was going on. I am forever grateful for friends like her who have led me back to Holy Spirit in times of crisis.

It took me a while to hear His voice. I remember just crying while people loudly experienced the joy of the Lord all around me. If you've ever been in that position, you know how awkward it can feel.

Then I heard Him ask if I knew what was upsetting me. I didn't really have words, so I said no. He then asked if I *wanted* to know—a question He asks me when He's about to share a hard truth.

I hesitantly said yes, and I'll never forget His response. He said, *"You're scared because you think that you're missing out on a part of Me, that you don't really know Me, and that I'm holding out on you."* There it was. The ugly truth that was causing me to writhe on the inside in that moment.

I asked Him to tell me the truth, and He did. He revealed to me that there will always be more to His presence, and that is a good thing. Forever and ever we will be exploring and enjoying His presence! He assured me I hadn't done anything wrong—I just hadn't experienced this manifestation of His Spirit yet. And He rather amusingly pointed out that obviously I *did* know Him because I was having a conversation with Him. (That got a chuckle out of me.)

He then reminded me that it's not His nature to hold anything back from His children. In fact, His nature was displayed on the cross where He held *nothing* back as He opened wide His arms and His heart to all humanity. He so succinctly quieted my fears that I suddenly felt at home again—in His presence—with or without the flopping drunkards all around me.

Then I felt His invitation. A proverbial hand extended, asking me to step into this crazy river. I remember thinking, *"I'm just not like these people. My personality is just not this joyful."* Immediately, I felt a Holy Spirit check and pause in my mental reasoning, an obvious indicator to me that He didn't agree with something I had just thought.

He whispered, *"Do you want* Me *to tell you about your personality since I'm the One who made you?"* I knew in that moment I was being invited to cross a threshold and move into a new thing with Him. I was still a little scared and awkwardly aware of my surroundings, but my heart said, *"Yes!"*

That *yes* led to one of the most profound encounters I'd had up to that point, which led to a *season* of encounters that changed me, from the inside out. He showed me the Throne Room, pulsating with light and life. People surrounded His throne as far as I could see, and the brightest light shone at the center of His throne.

When He asked me what I noticed about the people in that place, I knew in my spirit He was pointing out the immeasurable joy they all exhibited. He then said, *"No one is grumpy here!"* which suddenly seemed like the *funniest* thing I had ever heard, and before I knew it I was laughing uncontrollably!

A moment earlier, accepting the label of a melancholy personality seemed logical. Now it seemed down right hilarious! Over the following months, Holy Spirit encountered my heart and dismantled lies I had believed about myself and about Him, and He gave me the truth. I grew in confidence, character, and gifting. It felt like I was running on the mountains with Him, every day a new adventure. I am so thankful for that beautiful season of unusual encounters!

Months later, I came across the drawing I had made in my sketchbook of my heart as an overflowing fountain. Above the heart drawing were the words, "I want to give all that's inside of my heart to You," and I realized He was answering that cry. He was faithfully and lovingly opening my heart so I could truly give it *all* to Him.

GOD HONORS YOUR CHOICE

In retrospect, that initial moment of invitation was so important and obviously life-changing for me, but at the time it just felt like one small choice. In that season of encounter and growth, I had to let go of pride, fear, and shame as I waded deeper into His presence—which wasn't always easy.

Something that stood out to me, even more than the healings I saw in front of my eyes or the hearts set free, was the significance of *divine invitation*. Can you see it, too? He really does want to *partner* with us, but He always gives us a choice!

From the beginning, He gave us the extraordinary gift of free will, and He has never violated that decision. He always gives us a choice. While His invitations are glorious, we still have to say *yes* to experience the joy of running with Him. I can relate to the Shulamite in that when we experience the heart-pain of saying no to Him, our hunger for Him then must become stronger than our fear of the unknown. Whatever it takes, giving God your *yes* over and over is the most impactful thing you can do for your heart, your life, and your legacy.

THE MOMENT OF BUY-IN

I've always admired people who appear to live fearlessly. Those brave souls who summit mountains, deep sea dive, or jump out of airplanes. They may seem fearless, but I'm sure they would tell you that fear isn't absent; they simply learn to push past it. Creative process often possesses its own ledges and cliffs we must learn to jump from. When the execution stage is upon us, we experience the most resistance. This is where the yes in our hearts must be louder than the fears holding us back. There has to be buy-in.

Wanting the thing, thinking about the thing, researching the thing, buying supplies to do the thing, talking about the thing, telling others you're going to do the thing—none of that is actually *doing* the thing. Sometimes in an effort to be prepared for the thing we want, we end up forfeiting it as we wait for the perfect conditions. God doesn't have to wait for perfect conditions to move. *He* is perfect, therefore conditions bow to Him wherever He goes.

To that point, there is a long list of examples in the scripture of God taking a yielded heart, in *imperfect* conditions, and doing something completely new and astounding. Abraham simply took God at His word—without a discipleship training program, without scriptures to memorize, and without worship albums playing in his tent 24/7. He became the Father of Israel with no degree, no apprenticeship, no social media following—just God speaking to him in the night through the stars was enough for his heart to yield, to buy-in to God's plan and change the world.[2]

Moses is another great example. He was born into a political climate where the national leader was murdering babies for population control. He narrowly escaped his own demise only to be brought into that very leader's household as an adopted grandson until he was forced to flee into the desert as a fugitive for murdering an Egyptian.

Years later, while attending to his Father-in-law's flock in the desert, he came upon a burning bush, flaming with the consuming fire of God. The scripture records Moses saying, *"I will now turn aside and see this great sight, why the bush does not burn."*[3]

He chose to stop what he was doing and investigate the strange sight before Him. He "turned aside" from going his own way and answered the call of the infinite God. He said *yes* to the moment of invitation through which God raised up Israel's deliverer.

Noah was given direction from God to build a boat in order to survive a flood that was coming to cover the earth, and he had never seen rain before.[4] By all accounts, Noah had circumstance on his side to reason himself out of obedience, but he did not. He recognized God's invitation, said *yes*, and had the grace to execute it with diligence and accuracy. One man's *yes* to a seemingly crazy divine invitation, saved humanity. Your *yes*, big or small, matters.

Esther is one of my favorite examples, not only because she is a woman, but also because she had seen some things.[5] Life wasn't pretty for her—not as an orphan, nor among an exiled people, and not when she was brought into the king's harem. Her life was a story created by other people's choices and by unfortunate circumstances, and yet she did not harden her heart.

I wonder, if we were in her shoes, would we embrace the invitation to step into the unknown, risking life and limb, or would we hide behind the comfort of the palace and a title? God put the fate of the Jewish people in the hands of Esther, and her *yes to the invitation* was the key to their deliverance.

And there are many more examples:

- John *turns* toward the voice that was like a trumpet before the unveiling of Jesus.[6]
- Mary, whose entire life was changed in a moment, said *yes* to the angelic proclamation that she would birth the son of God despite the negative impact to her life.[7]
- The woman at the well was confronted by a man claiming to be the messiah who knew *"everything she's ever done."*[8] Instead of getting offended, as I imagine most of us would be if a stranger told us about our sin, she ran to her town and told everyone to come meet Him! She accepted Jesus's invitation to drink the Living Water and saves an entire village in the process! That's buy-in!
- Then there is the Shulamite[9] maiden who is the ultimate example of both accepting and declining the invitation of God.

In Song of Songs we read a beautiful love story between a Bridegroom King and a humble shepherdess referred to as the Shulamite. Through their unfolding tale, we are given such a beautiful picture of our relationship with Jesus.

The two fall in love and experience all the gooey sap of infatuation which we see in chapter one from the very first verse (TPT):

> *"Let him smother me with kisses—his Spirit-kiss divine. So kind are your caresses, I drink them in like the sweetest wine!"*

It's brooding and incubation through and through, and it is reminiscent of most born again believer's first season of walking with the Lord. Then in chapter two the Bridegroom King extends the sweetest invitation to come away and run with him.

"Arise, my dearest. Hurry, my darling. Come away with me! I have come as you have asked to draw you to my heart and lead you out. For now is the time, my beautiful one. The season has changed, the bondage of your barren winter has ended, and the season of hiding is over and gone. The rains have soaked the earth and left it bright with blossoming flowers. The season for singing and pruning the vines has arrived. I hear the cooing of doves in our land, filling the air with songs to awaken you and guide you forth. Can you not discern this new day of destiny breaking forth around you? The early signs of my purposes and plans are bursting forth. The budding vines of new life are now blooming everywhere. The fragrance of their flowers whispers, "There is change in the air." Arise, my love, my beautiful companion, and run with me to the higher place. For now is the time to arise and come away with me."

— Song of Songs 2:10-14, TPT

LEARNING TO SEE THE INVISIBLE

So how do we recognize an invitation from an invisible God? When Jesus extends invitations to us, it may not be this obvious, but His steady heart behind the call is the same as in these verses. He calls us to come out of hiding, to discern the hopeful possibilities all around us, and to embrace the opportunity to trust Him in the adventure of life.

The way most Christians talk, the only option to such an invitation is to accept with a heart full of faith and disregard for anything but God's glory. If that's your story, I applaud you, but sadly it isn't mine. And it wasn't the Shulamite's story either. She said no the first time. And surprisingly she declined not out of ignorance for who the Bridegroom King was or the sweetness of his love, but because of fear.

*"I know my lover is mine and I have everything in you, **for we delight ourselves in each other**. But until the day springs to life and **the shifting shadows of fear disappear**, turn around, my lover, and ascend to the holy*

*mountains of separation without me. Until the new day fully dawns, run on ahead like the graceful gazelle and skip like the young stag over the mountains of separation. Go on ahead to the mountain of spices—**I'll come away another time.***"

— SONG OF SONGS 2:16-17, TPT (EMPHASIS ADDED)

Notice how she is expressing her delight in the love that they have, but at the same time she is very aware of her fear of the shifting shadows that she sees lying ahead. It reminds me of the story I shared earlier. I was so content in the prayer room, delighting in our love, and Jesus stepped in and invited me into more. At first, all I saw were shifting shadows of uncertainty that clouded out the beauty of the invitation.

I wonder if you can relate. When we have reached the place where we can honestly and openly declare our love for Jesus, our areas of compromise become harder to recognize. Once we know we love Him our "nos" aren't usually outright "yeses" to sin or darkness. It's more often the seemingly small things—the lesser things—that keep us from the more of God. It's the sneaky dullness of familiarity that can cause us to take His presence for granted. We might find ourselves settling for things that are good, while saying no to God. It's often procrastination, laziness, and boredom caused by religion that snuff out the fire in the modern believer's heart. The Shulamite says something in her response to the Bridegroom King's invitation that, if we are honest, we probably say to Jesus more than we would like to admit—*I'll come away another time.*[10]

Have you ever been woken up in the night and felt a gentle tug to get up and talk to the Lord, yet you rolled over and dismissed it? Have you sensed Him highlighting a co-worker to you that you knew you were supposed to pray for and share the gospel with, and yet you reasoned your way out of it? Maybe there is a project you've put off, a class you never enrolled in, or a mission trip you've felt drawn to. The comfort of the experiences we've known can be a dangerous substitute for the abundant life that's available to us through partnership.

We must end our love affair with fear and comfort and let Perfect Love lead us out! If we don't say *yes* to the smaller daily invitations to lean into Him, we won't be prepared to say *yes* to the bigger ones.

Thankfully, we see in the next part of the story that even after the Shulamite rejects the Bridegroom King, he remains faithful to her. She can't seem to find him, and is restless in her search until she apprehends the one she loves. Have you ever experienced a time when you just ached and longed for His presence, but couldn't seem to find Him? I would propose that when we say *no* to the many seemingly small invitations of God, our own heart then condemns us and we withdraw from experiencing His presence! *We aren't designed to say no to Him; we are designed to run with Him!*

In chapter four the Bridegroom King comes back to express His love freely to her once again. This time, His presence satisfies her longing for Him in such a deep way that she immediately declares her desire to run with Him.

> *"I've made up my mind. Until the darkness disappears and the dawn has fully come, in spite of the shadows and fears, I will go to the mountaintop with you —the mountain of suffering love and the hill of burning incense. Yes, I will be your bride."*
>
> — Song of Songs 4:6, TPT

She doesn't deny the existence of the shadows and fears; she just decides she wants him more. What a beautiful declaration! Despite her *no,* His perfect love *did* indeed lead her out.

A few years ago I experienced this same dynamic with Jesus within a different context. I was a new mom with a two-year-old and a newborn...and tired, so very tired. Physically, my health was struggling, and I was experiencing anxiety and panic.

I hadn't painted in years, and I just didn't see the point anymore. It just all seemed too expensive, messy, time consuming—I barely had the energy to shower, so painting seemed laughable. During this difficult season, I struggled to hear God, especially for me personally. I was constantly aching for more and frustrated that He always seemed out of reach.

One afternoon after I got both babies down for a nap, I was cleaning the kitchen when my chest began to tighten, and I could feel panic gripping me. I sat on the floor and tried to breathe through the anxiety attack. I whispered a prayer for help and suddenly heard God speak so clearly for the first time in a while.

He invited me to start painting again. I wasn't confident I was hearing Him because it just seemed silly. I didn't see how painting had anything to do with how I was feeling. I needed a solution, not arts and crafts. Once I calmed down, I didn't really think about it anymore, until He brought it up again a few days later.

When He brought it up again, I was watching Bob Ross (an American painter and television personality who hosted the popular PBS show The Joy Of Painting from 1983-94) while the kids napped. The Lord whispered, *"You know, you could do that if you wanted."*

I just flat out didn't agree with Him. I had so many reasons why I thought that voice couldn't be God. Money was tight. I didn't have oil paints, and barely any other supplies. I didn't think I had the time or energy. It literally just felt like a terrible idea to even consider getting back into painting.

I decided to walk to the mailbox while I thought about God's strange invitation. An early birthday card with a check inside was waiting for me, and again I felt God's whisper, *"What are you going to do with that?"* In that moment, I decided that, despite the discomfort of the unknown, I would say *yes* to Him because I trusted Him.

After buying some oil paints and supplies, I began painting again during the times each day when my kids napped. Sometimes it was only a half hour, but something profound happened as I made it a priority and kept choosing to show up. I rediscovered my heart. My mind became clearer. My spirit was satisfied in His presence as I often experienced the sensation of Him just sitting in the room with me while I painted.

The creative process of painting realigned my heart to His and brought multi-dimensional healing to my life. Do I think this happened because painting is magic? No. I think it was helpful because it's what He *invited* me into. I'm so thankful I recognized that invitation, even though it seemed absurd, and that I accepted. Allowing creativity to have an intentional space again changed the trajectory and the overall enjoyment of my life.

After the invitation is recognized and accepted, you will get swept up into the execution stage. This is when what's been incubating on the inside begins to take form on the outside. Like the light bursting forth in Genesis, the execution stage gives outward expression for the hidden world of the heart. It's the baby being born after forming in the dark. It's the butterfly exiting the cocoon, a new creation. It's when your wings stretch out for the first time, and you begin to fly. It's the long awaited stage for you "doers" out there.

During the execution stage, there is excitement and adrenaline in the moment of stepping out and following His lead, but there are also new tests and pitfalls to be mindful of. We will talk about that next, but before we move on, take a minute to sit with Holy Spirit and ask Him these questions.

CHAPTER SUMMARY

- Learning to recognize and embrace God's invitations is the key to unlocking life-long adventure with Jesus and avoiding the spirit of religion.
- He always gives us a choice because He only wants voluntary lovers.

- God doesn't wait for perfect conditions to move. He is perfect, therefore circumstances must bow to Him.
- Your responses to God's invitations won't just affect your life —they will ripple throughout eternity.
- We must end our love affair with fear and comfort, and let perfect love lead us out.
- If we don't say *yes* to the small, daily invitations to lean into Him, we won't be prepared to say *yes* to the bigger invitations.
- We aren't designed to say *no* to Him; we are designed to run with Him.

QUESTIONS FOR REFLECTION

1. Looking back over your life, when can you remember God extending to you a clear personal invitation to run with Him?

2. Ask Holy Spirit if there are any open invitations currently in your life that He's waiting for your response to. If so, take some time to have an honest conversation with Him about it.

3. Process with Holy Spirit any times you have declined an invitation. What was the result? What happened next? Did it eventually present itself again? Take some time to acknowledge His goodness and faithfulness to you even in the midst of declined invitations and missed opportunities.

4. Ask the Holy Spirit how you can better recognize His invitations in your life. It is so important to hear and heed Holy Spirit's invitations. Think of a specific invitation from Him in your past. What did it feel like? What was unique about it compared to other times He speaks?

5. Sometimes we can decline invitations from the Lord without even realizing it. Is there anything your heart has expressed a desire for recently that might actually be the Lord's invitation?

––––––––––––––––––

1. Song of Songs 2:10-15 TPT "The one I love calls to me: Arise, my dearest. Hurry, my darling. Come away with me! I have come as you have asked to draw you to my heart and lead you out. For now is the time, my beautiful one. The season has changed, the bondage of your barren winter has ended, and the season of hiding is over and gone. The rains have soaked the earth and left it bright with blossoming flowers. The season for singing and pruning the vines has arrived. I hear the cooing of doves in our land, filling the air with songs to awaken you and guide you forth. Can you not discern this new day of destiny breaking forth around you? The early signs of my purposes and plans are bursting forth. The budding vines of new life are now blooming everywhere. The fragrance of their flowers whispers, "There is change in the air." Arise, my love, my beautiful companion, and run with me to the higher place. For now is the time to arise and come away with me. For you are my dove, hidden in the split-open rock. It was I who took you and hid you up high in the secret stairway of the sky. Let me see your radiant face and hear your sweet voice. How beautiful your eyes of worship and lovely your voice in prayer. You must catch the troubling foxes, those sly little foxes that hinder our relationship. For they raid our budding vineyard of love to ruin what I've planted within you. Will you catch them and remove them for me? We will do it together."
2. See Genesis 12.
3. See Exodus 3:3, NKJV.
4. See Genesis 6-9.
5. See the Book of Esther.
6. See Revelation 1:12.
7. See Luke 1:38.
8. John 4:29 Considered the New Testament's first evangelist, the woman at the well is one of the most beautiful stories of a life transformed in a moment, and then poured out for His glory.
9. See Song of Songs.
10. See Song of Songs 2:17.

CHAPTER 4

STAGE THREE: EXECUTION, OR THE ART OF ŠĀMA

"Don't just listen to the Word of Truth and not respond to it, for that is the essence of self-deception. So always let his Word become like poetry written and fulfilled by your life."

— James 1:22, TPT

"I have been impressed with the urgency of doing. Knowing is not enough; we must apply. Being willing is not enough; we must do."

— Leonardo Da Vinci

Hopefully you've noticed by now that God's creative process is fluid in nature. While the stages are distinct, they also overlap and sometimes play out at the same time. That dynamic actually makes writing this book difficult because describing God's ways and His Kingdom realm isn't always straight forward. It is difficult to explain something that must be experienced to be understood.

The execution stage of God's process is where things are caught, rather than taught. It's where we learn in the *doing* and discover a new part of God's heart in the process. This stage is exciting and full of adventure. It also carries its own version of resistance and tests that refine us on the journey.

DIVING IN

In discussing this stage, what I'm actually referring to is *any action that you are doing in response to the Lord's leading*. It's anything that requires *obedience*, that flesh killing act, in order to be accomplished. That obedience can be as small as painting with God or as big as praying to see the dead raised. It can be as mundane as doing household chores and as tedious as doing your taxes.

No matter what the action may be, if you are doing it with the Creator, it can be creative and fun. And I hope we can agree, in everything that we are *doing* with Him, we should be seeking to release His Kingdom and its ways. After all, we are the agents through whom He's chosen to release his Kingdom into the earth.

So don't get stuck on "execution" looking or sounding like a particular *activity*. This is more of a diving into the concepts, experiences, and implications of the stage itself. Let the execution stage become for you a philosophy of *doing everything in union* with God.

This is the stage I am, by nature, least prone to step into. If left to my own devices, I would likely float away into the land of ideas and never come down. I love ideas, thinking, learning, understanding, and processing, especially with Holy Spirit. When it comes to stepping out and *doing*, sometimes I need a bit of a shove.

In the art studio over these last five years or so, I have learned so much about the *doing*. I've learned that negative self-talk doesn't ever help us get anything done, and it should be dealt with *while it's happening*. I've also learned that the fastest way to kill negative inner dialogue is to ask Holy Spirit what He thinks, and then intentionally and *with your mouth* agree with Him. In other words, say what God is saying about yourself and your situation. It's that simple.

THE LIE OF "NOT ENOUGH"

The most persistent and common resistance I have experienced and witnessed in the art studio (and in life for that matter) is the idea that you are somehow not enough. This idea comes packaged and labeled in a lot of different ways:

- perfectionism
- comparison
- false humility
- fear of rejection
- fear of the opinion of others, etc.

But it all carries the same core lie that you're not enough.

This lie can trip you up for days, weeks, months, and years if you're not careful. I find it to be most pernicious just before moving into the execution stage. And if you manage to overcome that, it seems to reappear right as you are about to move from the execution stage into the evaluation stage. It's a lie we must reckon with, dismantle with the word of God, and let go of if we are to truly pursue a life of being *and* doing with God.

When teaching art, I encourage my students to talk about how they feel before, during, and after their creative process. I think becoming more aware of your internal world is an important part of learning your own creative process and discovering the roadblocks that are hindering you.

The tendency is to evaluate the art rather than the artist, but the artist is where the gold is. Students will inevitably want to tell me what they don't like about their art rather than how they feel or what they learned.

Creativity can be an emotional trigger because it pushes us outside our comfort zones. That sudden discomfort can be a shock if we weren't expecting it, and I have witnessed many students operating in self-judgment or false-humility as if it will alleviate the pain.

Experiencing discomfort during the creative process doesn't necessarily mean something is wrong. If you're not experiencing some level of discomfort in your creative endeavors, then it's safe to say you're not growing. Conversely, if you are being brave and stepping out into a new thing, then vulnerability will almost always uncover some opportunity for growth.

Another thing I have learned in the studio is that I can sit with my Bible in hand, enjoying God's presence and allowing Him to brood and lead our time together. Then as soon as the paintbrush is picked up, I can slip into my own strength with the assumption that *I must do this part on my own.*

Being with God is something that comes naturally to me, *doing* with Him is a whole other skillset. Your ear has to be so attuned, constantly listening, staying curious, obeying quickly. In essence, you are trying to follow the wind, and to do this you must fully engage your attention toward Him, leaving none to put on yourself.

WHEN THE CREATIVE PROCESS INTERSECTS WITH ANOINTING

I once experienced this dynamic in an unexpected place, on a ministry trip. A few summers ago, I had the honor of getting to travel with one of the senior leaders at my church on a ministry trip. It was a quick weekend trip, and flight delays and unexpected hiccups had our team finally meeting together only moments before the service was about to start.

I had never been on a trip like this and had no idea what to expect. I was feeling stretched and super vulnerable. Pastor Joaquin gave us direction to simply walk around the room during worship and anywhere that felt like it needed it, to just stand there and worship. In that moment, I was struggling to take my attention off of me, so I was feeling very inadequate.

Despite the nagging fear that I had nothing to offer to the team that night, I did what he said and walked around the room worshiping. As I did this my attention was obviously turned to the Lord and His presence. My awareness of His presence just kept growing, and I felt drunker and drunker as I soaked and allowed Him to brood.

Eventually, I was face down on the floor, unable to stand. While laying there, my thoughts wandered onto the night I first walked into the outpouring that I shared about in the previous chapter. I felt like God said to be ready to share about that experience.

I was so surrendered and steeped in His presence at that moment that I gave no thought to what that actually meant. The next thing I knew, I saw Pastor Joaquin standing on a chair calling out words of knowledge over the room into the microphone, and people were praying for one another and getting touched by God's presence. Then he got down and asked me if I had anything to share. I can not fully express to you how "out-of-body" that moment felt when I said *yes!*

He quickly introduced me and handed me the mic. I shared the story of walking into the awakening and feeling the invitation to step into the river. As I handed the mic back, he gleefully yelled the word *"transference"* at me, which had no meaning to me in that moment, and then invited anyone in the room that was feeling stirred for *more of God* to come to the front!

I'm laughing while I write this, remembering how full of God that moment was as what seemed like more than half the room rushed to the front in response to His call. I literally had no idea what to do and was beginning to be more aware of myself than God again. I'm sharing these details because, again, I think that while self-awareness is important, losing awareness of yourself is key when we are intentionally trying to partner with God.

Joaquin headed to the side of the room and gestured for me to follow him. Watching him flow in that moment was so incredible as he partnered with what He saw God doing in the room. He said to me, "*You're going to pray for them!*"

I was now starting to feel painfully sober as I awkwardly stepped up to the first woman in line for prayer. I put my hands on hers and closed my eyes as I was accustomed to do. Inside I was begging Jesus to come through in that moment. Pastor Joaquin was behind me, and he whispered, "Grace," then quickly stepped in closer and blew on the woman. She immediately fell out in God's presence!

My awareness of God's presence instantly increased, and I understood how Joaquin was instructing me in that moment. I needed to move in *grace*, stay attuned to God's Spirit, and obey quickly. When I was more aware of my weakness than God's presence, I began to strive in my own strength, thinking *I had to do this part on my own*. I was trying to do *for* Him, not *with* Him.

I stepped over to the next person to pray for them. Joaquin instructed me to do *quick* prayers. Unexpectedly, we then both did the same gesture towards the next person, somehow now tuned into the same frequency, and they fell out, too! This repeated down the line as I surrendered to Holy Spirit's lead and followed in obedience.

I just did what I saw in the Spirit, not unlike how I paint. The "more of God" I was carrying was indeed transferring to these hungry brothers and sisters, and I was just the gateway.[1] I learned so much that night about partnering with God by watching someone who had developed this skill over years, and I had so much fun doing it!

I want you to know that praying for a line of people and watching them topple like dominoes is not normal for me, nor has it ever really been a desire. Partnering with God, however, has very much been a desire of my heart for years. I had seen others move in this type of ministry, and I have been one of those dominoes before, but never had

I been so filled and confident in the Lord as I was that night ministering in God's grace.

There were many lessons that night, but the thing that stood out was that the more surrendered I was to *His* ways and the less concerned I was with getting it right, the easier His spirit seemed to move. *In other words, the more I was able to get out of the way, the more room He had to come through.* I don't know about you, but that is something I want in my life all the time!

As I processed later with God in complete awe of what He did that night, He explained to me that what I experienced was *anointing.* He was able to move through me that night and touch those hungry people because I was partnering with Him. I was allowing Him to lead and was not worrying about my inadequacies.

Finding this Holy Spirit led current is the heart of the execution stage, and I believe it is the sweet spot for image bearers. It is the place where our unique creative process intersects with His anointing.

I learned something profound that night about myself and about my Creator. He's always looking for ways to release His life into hearts. He seeks gateways through which His glory can come through. Whether the vehicle looks like a canvas, a book, a homeschool lesson, or a prayer line, He wants us with Him *doing* what He does. He wants us running with Him.

He's proud of every *yes* we give and all of our awkward first steps as we learn to walk in step with Him, but I also believe He is especially proud when we lose sight of our weakness or inadequacy and begin to boldly execute from under the shadow of His wings.

THE ART OF ŠĀMA AND THE SPIRIT OF WISDOM

When I think about people throughout history who have exhibited an unusual grace on their lives for creativity and execution, two people stand out to me. King Solomon of the Bible and Leonardo Da Vinci.

Both were incredibly prolific and seemed to execute creatively with wisdom that wasn't common on the earth in their generation.

Da Vinci was a painter, draftsman, sculptor, architect, and engineer whose skill and intelligence (perhaps more than that of any other figure) epitomized the name Renaissance.[2] Solomon was a king, a poet, an architect, and the wealthiest man in the world in his time. I believe King Solomon's life, above any other, contains profound secrets into understanding and executing the creative process of God in the earth.

Solomon's name is often synonymous with wisdom due to the conversation he had with God and the books of wisdom he penned.[3] That special conversation with God is mentioned in two places, 2 Chronicles 2 and 1 Kings 3. Solomon famously asks for wisdom, an understanding heart, and the ability to judge and lead the people. The word used for "understanding heart" is *šāma* which is often translated as "wisdom."[4] It's like wisdom because it's the ability to understand, but it also involves the ability to act upon that understanding with obedience—to partner your *yes* with understanding. The idea here isn't just being smart, although intelligence is a part of it. It's having a heart that understands the ways of God and *specifically* the ability to execute His ways.

Solomon was considered the wisest of men because he was able to make sound judgments and lead his people in a way the world hadn't seen before. He was also incredibly prolific. He was responsible for building the temple, writing multiple books of the Bible, penning over 3,000 proverbs, and composing over 1,000 songs. His success as a leader and the wealth of the nation at the time of his reign was unparalleled.

What made him stand apart? I believe it is what he asked for: a listening and understanding heart to the ways of God. If we want to partner with the Creator in life, asking for an understanding heart and grace to obey is a great place to start.

The ways of God aren't like ours.[5] It takes *revelation* to understand his ways. His ways, or more simply put, how God chooses to do things, are righteous by definition—*the very Spirit of Wisdom*. It is woven into the fabric of creation. It's the way He thinks and processes. It's expressed in the balance of all creation—from the cosmos to the atoms that form your body.

How God chooses to do things—*His ways*—are perfect, and there is an open invitation for us to learn His ways and implement them into the fabric of our lives. We may not have forty thousand horses like Solomon or receive visits from royalty seeking to understand the secret to His success, but we have the same invitation to a relationship with the Creator as He did!

Another person in the Bible who possessed such a spirit is Bezalel. In Exodus 31 he is mentioned as one of the artisans God called and anointed to create the garments for the priests and the items for the tabernacle. Incidentally, he is the first person in scripture that God says He put His spirit *in*.

> *"Now the Lord said to Moses, "See, I have called by name Bezalel, the son of Uri, the son of Hur, of the tribe of Judah. And I have filled him with the Spirit of God in wisdom and skill, in understanding and intelligence, in knowledge, and in all kinds of craftsmanship, to make artistic designs for work in gold, in silver, and in bronze, in the cutting of stones for settings, and in the carving of wood, to work in all kinds of craftsmanship."*
>
> — Exodus 31:1-5, AMP

How interesting that the first person mentioned in scripture to have God's Spirit in them, rather than upon them, is an artist. In fact, a couple chapters before God said, "*So you shall speak to **all who are gifted artisans**, **whom I have filled with the spirit of wisdom**, that they may make Aaron's garments, to consecrate him, that he may minister to Me as priest.*"[6]

There is a special relationship between artists and the spirit of wisdom. For these artisans, the divine commission *had* to involve anointing. They couldn't google "how to make an ephod." They had to receive that instruction and understanding from God. How much more is that true now for us who have the Holy Spirit living in us?

Why was Bezalel bestowed with such an honor? Why was he chosen? We aren't really told, but God gives us a clue when He called him by name. So I was curious—what does Bezalel's name mean? It means *In the shadow of God!* His very name was a prophecy. He was overshadowed by the Creator and filled with His spirit.

Another clue is when God said, *"I have filled Him with the Spirit of God."*[7] What name did God use for Himself here? Elohim, the same name for God in Genesis when He's creating everything. In essence, God was saying I have filled him with the Spirit of the Creator!

What if we *all* sought to live in the shadow of God, filled and in-step with the Spirit of The Creator? What could we execute with Him in that place?

OTHER LESSONS FROM THE EXECUTION STAGE

The Execution Stage is the part of the creative process that others see. It can be doing the painting, writing the book, or recording the album. It can also be the moment you step out to share a word of knowledge, pay for the coffee of the customer behind you in line, or call your estranged loved one as the Lord leads.

It's the moment when the process you've been in with God is suddenly on the outside of you. It's a moment of reckoning of sorts because this is when other people's opinions become a part of the process. Their praise and rejection are a test. Your success and your failure are a test. It's a litmus test that will reveal the fruit that was planted in the incubation. Whether you experience success or failure in the execution stage, both have the ability to reveal what's most important to your heart. In that regard, both success and failure are valuable.

For example, you can get the thing you thought you always wanted only to immediately realize it's not what you thought it was. I experienced this during my first art showing in a gallery. It started when I had whispered a desire of my heart to the Lord in the secret place. I asked if I could one day show my art in a gallery in NYC.

At the time, the request felt larger than life, and I was almost embarrassed to ask. Fast forward a few years, and my first gallery invitation came, and guess where it was? New York City. The show just happened to fall on my spiritual birthday, and as I walked into the gallery to view my work front and center, I heard Him whisper, "Happy Birthday."

I knew intuitively in that moment the gallery show was nothing compared to the experience of knowing Jesus. The One who shot a star across the sky and sat next me on the beach was the gift that mattered most. The "success" of getting the thing I thought I wanted more than anything revealed the invaluable thing I already had!

Often the experience of "doing the thing," whatever it may be, is not nearly as interesting as we imagined it to be. That's because execution is just part of life; it's not life in its entirety. Perhaps one of the easiest ways to miss your life is to wait around believing you won't be fully alive "until." Until you get married, get pregnant, get that promotion, lose the extra weight, get to enjoy retirement, and so on.

There are so many "untils" that will steal our lives away. It is a fantasy to wait around for the next exciting execution stage—the next big thing— only to be continually confronted with the reality that our souls crave so much more than the execution stage alone can give us. Our souls long for the intimacy with our Creator that's found when we intentionally engage in life with Him. If we sell ourselves short and live for a lesser thing, we are destined to experience a string of disappointments and bitterness.

In reality, the execution moments of life, when something *big* is happening, is really only about 5% of the entirety of our existence. It is a valuable 5%, but it won't fill you like learning to enjoy and deeply value the other 95%. That's where the meat of life lies—the still, quiet moments when no one is looking but your Creator. That's where you discover His heart as well as your own heart. That's where you learn to love Him as well as yourself.

If we don't find the value in the quiet in between moments, we can live in danger of thinking the next execution moment will "change everything." But the truth is, wherever you go, there you are. You are you whether you happen to be in a brooding stage or an execution stage. Even if you get that perfect job, spouse, or ministry opportunity —you're still you.

If you don't learn to love *you* (like Jesus does) and enjoy life with Him in the mundane moments of the brooding stages, then you won't enjoy or appreciate the execution moments either. Because the execution stage isn't the place where anything changes—that's what the cocoon was for.

FINALLY TAKING FLIGHT

Assuming you have allowed the cocoon to do its job and your insides have been transformed to align with Jesus, stretching out your new wings and taking flight can just be downright terrifying. I wouldn't presume to diminish that reality or insult you with some formula for overcoming the fear. Rather, my advice to you, after having jumped out of several cocoons for the first time myself, is to acknowledge the fear as a sign post that you are being brave, and then just do it. Do it scared if you have to.

Know that God is so deeply and unbelievably gracious, and recognize that mistakes are expected in the creative process. Be open to feedback—from God and others. Learn from your mistakes. Don't avoid conflict on or off the canvas!

What I mean is, don't hide from yourself. Determine in your heart to be *relentlessly* transparent with yourself and Jesus. Talk about *everything* with God. He is listening. He is gracious, slow to anger, abounding in love. He loves to give wisdom and does so generously. Once you know this about His nature and once you believe it, you won't hustle for revelation, wisdom, or anointing. If you know your Father's heart is to give you everything you need for life in godliness, then just ask Him for the desires of your heart.

The gold in the execution process is found in the mistakes, missteps, and missed opportunities. Those lessons aren't a part of the brooding. It takes a bold and brave heart. As you are courageously standing in your belovedness, willing to make mistakes, and in love with the One you are following, you will unearth that gold. *So get digging!* Do the brave thing everyday. Embrace the vulnerability of loving God and loving yourself, and you'll be ready to fly when it's time!

CHAPTER SUMMARY

- The Execution Stage can look like any action you are taking in response to the Lord's leading.
- "Not enough" is a lie that needs to be dismantled in order to live a life of being AND doing with God.
- Being with God and doing with Him can feel like two different skill sets.
- Anointing flows when we choose to operate in grace rather than our own strength.
- "Šāma" is the ability to understand *paired* with the grace to obey and execute.
- Bezalel lived under God's shadow and partnered with the Spirit of the Creator.
- Wherever you go, there you are. You are you in every stage of the process—so learn to love yourself and your life now!
- Don't hide from yourself in the Brooding Stage, and you'll have nothing to hide in the Execution Stage.

QUESTIONS FOR REFLECTION

1. Process with Holy Spirit through a time when you had fun partnering with Him. Write it out. Ask Him His perspective. Ask for more opportunities to "do the thing."

2. Do you find yourself rushing into the Execution Stage or avoiding it? Depending on your answer, ask the Holy Spirit for a plan to stretch yourself.

3. What's the scariest thing you can think of doing in partnership with Holy Spirit? Process with Him by asking: What is scary about it? What is exciting about it? Holy Spirit, what is Your perspective?

---

1. See Psalm 24:7.
2. "Leonardo Da Vinci." Encyclopædia Britannica. Encyclopædia Britannica, inc. Accessed November 9, 2021. https://www.britannica.com/biography/Leonardo-da-Vinci.
3. See 2 Chronicles 1 and 1 Kings 3.
4. Lexicon Strong's 8085.
5. "For *as* the heavens are higher than the earth, So **are My ways higher than your ways**, And My thoughts than your thoughts." Isaiah 55:9, NKJV
6. See Exodus 28:3 NKJV.
7. See Exodus 31:1.

CHAPTER 5

STAGE FOUR: EVALUATION + BLESSING = MOMENTUM

"The Lord bless you and keep you;
the Lord make his face to shine upon you
and be gracious to you;
the Lord lift up his countenance upon you
and give you peace."

— Numbers 6:24-26, NKJV

"*E*valuation plus blessing equals momentum.*" This is what the Lord said to me when I asked Him why He stops to tell us His thoughts about His creation in Genesis 1-2.

Have you ever considered the implications of God evaluating the works of *His* hands? Almost every day of creation He closes with some form of evaluation of His handiwork and with His blessing. I mean, was there ever any question about whether or not it was good? Everything He makes is good, for He *is* goodness!

God took the time to look at what He made, to consider what He thought about it, and to bless it out loud. If this act of evaluating wasn't about a judgment of the quality of His work, then what was the heart behind His evaluation? (*Because we know there is no question about quality when the Master Artist is* goodness!) And what was the purpose of putting it in the text for us to read?

I believe His heart was to look for the good because that is the Father's nature. And choosing to speak out the blessings was a vehicle to release momentum. Hebrews 1:3 (TPT) says, "*...He holds the universe together and expands it by the mighty power of his spoken word...*" His spoken words created everything from nothing. They hold all of creation together and somehow mysteriously release the expanding momentum of the universe. Evaluating and speaking blessing out loud is a divine model for releasing life. As His children, we carry a similar ability to speak life or death.[1]

EVALUATING LIKE THE FATHER

I believe the stages of the Creator's process in Genesis can serve as a blueprint for how His creation functions. The fourth stage in the creative process laid out in Genesis requires a process of stepping away from the proverbial canvas. It involves taking the time to observe what you have made, evaluating it, blessing it, and deciding if you're finished.

The invitation to move from execution into evaluation might be circumstantial, but learning to recognize the need to step back and evaluate is a valuable skill that comes with time and intention. It's so common to neglect this step.

We are often anxious about what we will see when we stand back, but what if there is another way to view this stage of evaluation? What if it's unto more life, beauty, and creative flow being released?

> "*God saw that the light was good (pleasing, useful) and He affirmed and sustained it; and God separated the light [distinguishing it] from the darkness.*

And God called the light day, and the darkness He called night. And there was evening and there was morning, one day."

— Genesis 1:4, AMP

The Father's evaluations and blessings might seem small, but consider the source.[2] When God says something is good, it's like Einstein calling someone smart. We might throw the word *good* around to describe all manner of things, but when God says it, it carries much more weight.

Obviously, this is because He is *God* and the very definition of goodness. Or, maybe less obviously, His words carry the most weight over us because He created us. We carry authority over the things we create. Our thoughts and words concerning those things are not separate from the tools we used to create them. It's all part of the process. Just like the Father, our evaluations aren't meant to be a judgment, but rather part of the creative process that releases more life.

During the season, when I realized our evaluation and blessing are part of the creative process, I was in the habit of being stingy with my praise of anything but Jesus. At the time, I often didn't think—and I certainly did not *say*—anything positive about a painting until it was finished. I guess my thinking was I shouldn't call it *"good"* if it's not finished, but I can't help but notice that doesn't line up with how God creates. He evaluates and blesses His creation by calling it good *while it's in process!* As you process that, beloved, make sure to remember that *you* are His creation that is in process too!

I've observed in my creative journey, and also in many of my students, a propensity for focusing on what we don't like and a resistance to acknowledging what we love. In all of my art classes, before my students leave I encourage them to clear their head from the image they wanted to create. I ask each student to stand in front of their paintings and ask the Lord what He thinks of it and to say *out loud* what they love about it.

Sometimes this is a simple process and a positive way to end a painting session, but for some it can be emotional and profound. Often, our evaluation of ourselves and our evaluation of the work of our hands is meshed on some level. Leaning in to hear His evaluation of you and the work separately creates a perfect opportunity to have a conversation with Holy Spirit about where your evaluations differ from His. Or better yet, just lay aside your ill-formed opinions and agree with your Creator.

Possibly one of the hardest things about the creative process for us to master is the step of evaluation and blessing, but was it always so hard? When we are young, it's natural and healthy to love the work of our hands. One of my favorite parts of being a mom is watching my kids create. Since my daughter was old enough to hold a crayon, she will stick her tongue out the side of her mouth without noticing when she's really lost in her creations. It is one of the sweetest most innocent things I've ever seen—her precious, deep blue eyes laser-focused on the stick figures she forges to symbolize her whole world, her family. Even at the age of three, I would see her give her all to creating, even engaging with her whole being. This is evidence we are all co-creators by birthright, not by training.

When she finally looked up at me as I watched her, her natural inclination was to proudly show me her creation. When she'd tell me about it, I would feel the presence of God increase in the room. It was precious and holy. I felt the need to be intentional in how I responded to her because this sweet stage of unbridled self-love is often unlearned because of the critique of others.

So many of us carry around wounds in the area of creativity because of someone else's, or our own, negative assessments. A caretaker or teacher's hurtful words about a child's artwork might seem like a small thing, but when they land in the rich, fertile soil of a young child's heart, they can wreak havoc for years to come.

The good news though is if negative self-evaluation is a learned behavior, it can be unlearned! Learning to evaluate and bless yourself and the work of your hands—just like Your heavenly Father does—can undo all those wounds and even empower you to help others!

BLESSING LIKE THE FATHER

An evaluation becomes a blessing when you speak it out loud. If we are brave enough to be kind to ourselves with our thoughts, it is another level of bravery to speak those thoughts out loud. Blessing, biblically speaking, isn't just saying something nice. Blessings are what a Father or Mother offers to their children to create momentum in their lives. It gives permission, opens up possibilities, and empowers them to run the path laid out before them.

The Father of everything took time to bless His creation along the way by speaking His evaluations out loud. Likewise, we get to offer that precious gift to the things we have authority over. This can be as surface level as saying kind things about what you create—whether it's a painting, a short story, or even a well-cooked meal. It can also be as profound as seeing the "gold" in your children and choosing to call it out in the midst of their stumbling through life.

One of the stories that comes to mind on this topic of blessing is the story of Jacob and Esau.[3] They were twins born to Issac and Rebekah. They were very different from each other, and they each found favor with a different parent—Esau with Isaac and Jacob with Rebekah.

When they were born, Esau was technically first and therefore had rights as the firstborn that Jacob didn't. One day Esau came in from hunting and wanted the soup Jacob was cooking. Jacob offered the soup in exchange for the birthright of the firstborn.

Esau didn't value his birthright and the blessing of his father that would be given exclusively to him, so he carelessly traded it in that moment for food. His short-sightedness cost him and his lineage bitterly, for he didn't receive the birthright blessing of Isaac. Instead, Jacob received it, and that blessing released momentum into his life for generations to come.

Though I have always been fascinated with this dynamic of a Father's blessing, the application of this story in modern times has often eluded me. It wasn't until writing this chapter that it finally clicked. When we partner with the Father in His evaluation of ourselves and our work, and we speak out loud the blessing in alignment with His heart, we receive the momentum that's released.

Sometimes we have to fight for that alignment and stand in faith until our sight is made new. And sometimes we don't understand the immense value of our birthright as an image bearer. Like Esau, we treat it with contempt and don't put on Heaven's perspective. We, too, trade our birthright for a bowl of soup when we don't learn to think like our Father.

If we don't value the blessing, we can forfeit the momentum of our life for the momentary comfort of false humility or criticism. It might feel uncomfortable to reorient your thinking and start speaking blessings over yourself and the work of your hand, but if you don't, you're giving up the divine potential that was offered to you at birth!

GLORY TO GLORY—THE MOMENTUM OF THE FATHER

I want to be clear. When I say *momentum*, I'm not talking about some shallow version of it that looks like the world's version of success. When I say *momentum*, I mean the flowing river of life that comes from your innermost being through your relationship with the Holy Spirit.[4]

The Bible often refers to our hearts being like a fountain or a river. We are meant to have His life flowing through us. When momentum is halted, it's like throwing a bunch of boulders in that river and damming up the waters of your life.

Water that doesn't flow becomes stagnant. In terms of a river that's meant to flow through you as a co-creator, those stagnant waters won't just limit life, they will invite death. The lifeless water metastasizes as anxiety, depression, and sickness of heart.

We were made to be givers of life, like God, and part of guarding the health of our hearts is guarding the evaluations we make and the words we speak out of those evaluations. The blessings we offer—in agreement with the Father—carry His power to open up a space ahead of us and move us into it.

Momentum, in scientific terms, is the force that keeps an object moving until friction stops it. I have found there is always some level of friction in the creative process because we are in a fallen world that resists The Creator.

In Heaven this friction doesn't exist. That's why evaluation and blessing ALONG THE WAY are so important for us on earth. Blessing is like a lubricant in the spirit that helps everything continue moving forward, reducing friction and maintaining momentum. In Psalm 133, God says He gives His blessing when He sees brothers and sisters dwelling in unity. He compares it to the oil, a natural lubricant, dripping down the beard of the high priest Aaron.

God didn't wait until the end of the week to evaluate His work, and you shouldn't wait until the end of your life to ask the Father about what *He* thinks of you. You can choose now to agree with Him and release the momentum of *His life* flowing through *your life!* In this way, engaging with holy evaluation and blessing is a sacrifice of praise that can only be offered this side of Heaven where friction still tries to restrict His life flow to us, in us, and through us.

HUMILITY IS AGREEMENT WITH GOD

Fighting to agree and partner with God's evaluation and blessings is a skill learned over time through repetition, and you will experience opposition along the way, both from within and without. Not only is it easier to see the things you don't like in yourself or your work, but in certain circles it is encouraged as a form of Christian humility.

This ideology says that acknowledging your accomplishments or the beauty you carry equates to pride and taking glory from God. We tend to think of humility as the opposite of arrogance, but true humility *is agreement with God.* This may go without saying, but you can always trust His assessments of you and your work because He *always* tells the truth.

During the outpouring season I mentioned in earlier chapters, God walked me through a year-long process of learning how to take thoughts captive and bring them into agreement with His heart. In essence, I was learning how to evaluate myself like He does.

Every time He would point out a lie I was believing about myself, He would then tell me the truth. The simple act of speaking out loud my agreement with His truth in place of the lie would produce change in my life from the inside out. While this process was so obviously changing how I thought, felt, and functioned in my everyday life, for a while I still struggled to really embrace an elevated view of myself.

I wondered how one could still walk in humility and simultaneously believe they were God's favorite. (Because we all are!) Then the Father redefined my understanding of humility.

Humility isn't thinking little of yourself or making sure you aren't arrogant. True humility is agreement with God, no matter what He says. If you confuse humility with false humility, this untruth will interrupt your ability to evaluate and bless rightly, hindering the potential momentum of your life.

Joseph, the son of Jacob, is a great example of this principle.[5] He had dreams in which God showed him symbolic pictures of being exalted above his eleven brothers and even his mother and father. I've heard it preached that Joseph was arrogant to share those dreams with his brothers, inflaming their jealousy which drove them to sell him as a slave. I'm not sure that's accurate. His brothers definitely *thought* he was being arrogant, and their wrong evaluation greatly altered the momentum of their entire family's future.

I don't know about you, but I don't think it was the brothers' evaluation I would want to be aligned with in this story. In contrast to their critical judgments, in humility, Joseph chose to believe God. He chose to continue believing God even when circumstances didn't line up with what he believed God was saying. That alignment with the Father and humility of heart kept Joseph on the path of favor and momentum while his brothers struggled to stay alive.

Joseph remained humble before God, and God remained faithful with Joseph. Even the great evil of his brothers' betrayal that was meant to destroy him, God used for good. I believe Joseph's amazing turn-around and miraculous promotion to the very pinnacle of earthly success had to do with his heart posture of humility. His victory? He simply agreed with God.

Let's sit with that for a minute. *Humility is agreement with God.* What could be more prideful than disagreeing with the One who made you, died for you, sustains you, and chases after your heart daily? Yet we do it all the time! Consider these God-spoken truths right now, and ask yourself if you agree with them wholeheartedly or if you uncon-sciously place conditions on them:

- *"I thank you, God, for making me so mysteriously complex!..."*[6]
- *"We have become His poetry..."*[7]
- *"Every part of you is so beautiful, my darling, Perfect is your beauty, without flaw within."*[8]
- *"God surveyed all he had made and said, "I love it!" For it pleased him greatly..."*[9]

Often we read scriptures like these and think something along the lines of, *"Wow, God is so good to love like that,"* or *"He loves me despite me."* But that's not really agreement with Him, is it? It is actually deflection. If He looks at you, the work of *His* hands, and declares how lovely you are, you should simply receive that and agree. Like-wise, you should be looking for the good like your Father does, calling it out and allowing yourself to enjoy the works of your hands!

MOMENTUM CARRIES INTO ETERNITY

There will be places in this life where we feel small, unimportant, incapable, or unwilling to go on. What we say and think over ourselves and the works of our hands in those moments of reckoning will determine the path we take from there. Our evaluation and blessing is what inspires momentum for us to continue on the narrow path that is sometimes difficult to stay on, the path of suffering love that the Shulamite learns to travel with her Bridegroom.

This chosen path isn't a fairytale. It's exactly what it sounds like, suffering love. Sometimes love involves sacrifice. This can look like a lot of different things, but the sacrifice of praise is one of the most important love offerings we get to give the Lord in this short life!

Choosing to praise when it's difficult, when you don't feel like it, when it seems life has not rewarded you for your risk, vulnerability, or bravery—that's when it matters most! That's when your praise is most potent!

We normally think of this concept only in terms of praising God, but it also applies to calling out the good in yourself and in your creations. When we get to Heaven, we will praise Him with unveiled faces, and it will be glorious. But it is *only* here on *this side* of Heaven that we can offer the praise through the pain. Through the veil, without sight, our praise when we can't see the full picture is an offering that releases life!

The same holds true when we exchange the lenses we've grown accustomed to viewing ourselves and our work through for God's perfect sight. When we choose to call out what is good, our words become a fountain of life. When we intentionally choose to bless the canvas in front of us, in whatever form it may be, no matter the stage of development, we are creating a path forward with momentum to continue the work until it is what it's supposed to be.

CHAPTER SUMMARY

- The Father always looks for the good in what He's made. We should follow suit.
- The Father blesses what He's made by speaking His evaluations out loud. We should follow suit.
- Everything came forth from His words, and His words sustain us. As His children, we carry a similar ability to speak life or death.
- We carry authority over the things we create.
- Our evaluations and blessings are not judgments, but rather one of the tools we use to create.
- God evaluates and blesses while the work is still in process.
- Learning to evaluate and bless yourself like Your heavenly Father does can heal creativity wounds and empower you to help others!
- When we partner with the Father in His evaluation of ourselves and our work and speak out loud the blessing in alignment with His heart, we receive the momentum that's released.
- When momentum is halted, it's like throwing a bunch of boulders in a river and damming up the waters of your life.
- True humility is agreement with God, no matter what He says.

SELF-TALK ACTIVATION

For this activation I want you to write a letter to yourself from the Father. Take as much time as you need. The words might flow freely and fiercely, or they might feel more like a trickle. Don't judge yourself harshly as you do this, rather simply engage with it for as long as there is grace. Then read it aloud to yourself. Consider reading it aloud to yourself everyday for a season, and journal how you feel about what you heard Him say. Address any area of disagreement that may come up.

If you have trouble receiving the words as felt truth, consider doing something creative with your letter. Sing it over yourself. Turn the key words into a mixed media piece of art. Write a story about a Father writing letters to His children. Ask Holy Spirit what your heart needs to help transfer His words of life from your head to your heart through your hands!

LET'S PRAY

Father, thank You for each one who will choose to engage with this exercise. I pray that Your words of life would come to the surface and flow through them. As a co-creator, I stand in agreement with Your evaluation of these precious ones and say that they are a raging river of life! I bless them to receive Your evaluations and agree with those evaluations all the days of their life. Today is a day of new beginnings and dams being dismantled in their spirit. Today is a day for momentum to be released that will be carried into eternity. Amen.

DEAR _____,

I'm writing you today because I want you to know that when I think about you, I think of

---

1. "Your words are so powerful that they will kill or give life, and the talkative person will reap the consequences." Proverbs 18:21 TPT
2. See Genesis 1:4, 1:10.
3. See Genesis 25:19-34.
4. John 4:14 TPT "but if anyone drinks the living water I give them, they will never thirst again and will be forever satisfied! For when you drink the water I give you it becomes a gushing fountain *of the Holy Spirit*, springing up and flooding you with endless life!"
5. See Genesis 37.
6. See Psalm 139:14, TPT.
7. See Ephesians 2:10, TPT.
8. See Song of Songs 4:7, TPT.
9. See Genesis 1:31, TPT.

CHAPTER 6

STAGE FIVE: REST

"By the seventh day, God had completed creating his masterpiece, so on the seventh day, he rested from all his work. So God blessed the seventh day and made it sacred, because on it, he paused to rest from all his work of creation."

— GENESIS 2:2-3, TPT

This has been the hardest chapter for me to write, and I didn't see that coming. I love to rest. I love sleep. I love going slow. My husband often teases me about the pace at which I would live life if I didn't have goals and deadlines (or a super, kind, go-getter husband) to help me along.

I know what rest looks like for me, and it usually means resting *from something.* However, the rest we see in Genesis 2 is a different beast. God wasn't taking a break from something when He chose to rest on the seventh day, but rather, He paused to *enjoy something.* The kind of rest that is a part of God's creative process isn't passive, or even just restorative. It's savoring. It's the Selah.

THE SAVORING GOD

When the Father takes His first "day off," it overlaps with humanity's first day of life. It was our orientation, so to speak, into this life—and The Father didn't hand Adam a to-do list. He rested with Him. He enjoyed life with him. This is the foundational, relational experience Adam had with the Father that he built his life upon. Just like we don't stop creating in order to evaluate and bless—evaluation and blessing are stages *within* the creative process—so, too, rest is an important stage. We often think of creating only in terms of the execution stage, but the Creator shows us in Genesis 1-2 that evaluation, blessing, and rest are all just as important as executing and brooding. Rest begets more life when done with the right spirit, the sabbath spirit.

Choosing to integrate sabbath rhythms into our daily cadence is one of the keys to unlocking abundant life and creative flow. In chapter three, I shared the story of when God invited me to start painting again. At the time I was struggling with panic attacks, living my life like a giant to-do list and then crashing the moment the people around me weren't in need of something.

When I started painting again, I had to intentionally carve out time in my life to create. I had to make preparations so that I wouldn't have excuses when it came time to paint. In a way, it became a place of true soul-rest. For that brief window of time, I wasn't concerned with doing for the purpose of feeling productive; I was simply playing for no other reason than enjoyment, and it filled me up every time! This is the kind of rest God brings us into.

That daily painting time was a place of rest for me, and my need for it grew over time. It eventually became a need for a whole, committed sabbath day. As a mom and primary care-giver throughout the week, my husband and I had to communicate about what sabbath was going to look like for me. I didn't have a standard job like him that I got a break from on the weekends, so it was going to take teamwork to make it happen.

Together, we decided that I didn't have to cook anything on Saturdays, which meant either he was cooking or we would eat leftovers. I wasn't allowed to clean on Saturdays. Also, I could sleep in that day if the kids woke up before us, and he would get up and get things going for our family. We also decided that we wouldn't use screens that day as much as possible, and we would go outside and do something fun together as a family—something we could lose track of time doing. I am so thankful for that season and the impacts of those sabbath rests on my health in body, soul, and spirit.

If your church day looks as busy as a weekday due to ministry serving commitments, then you need another day to be your sabbath day. Daily, weekly, even yearly, sabbath rests should be worked into our lives to maintain the health of our hearts.

In Leviticus 25 we read that even the land is supposed to have a sabbath in the jubilee year to revive the soil and allow for continued maximum harvest. It's rest that protects the flow of life for future generations. This is more evidence that the blueprint given in Genesis 1-2 shows us His process and the conditions under which we function best. Just like the land, our heart needs sabbath rests to be fertile and fully functional, and to protect the creative flow of life that is meant to flow from it.

THE SPIRIT OF THE SABBATH

We are His masterpiece, and in any great work of art it's not just the strokes of color that create the image—it's the negative space as well. It's the spaces, or moments of rest, in between the strokes that give shape and definition to the work. Without negative space, you'd simply have a block of color—a paint swatch.

Similarly, in music, it's not just the notes themselves, but the silence, that informs the listener. Rest creates space in-between sounds that draws the ear in a certain direction. They create emphasis and tell the story, as it were. In order to shine as the masterpiece He made us to be, we must allow rest to have its place in the melodies of our life.

If God can rest, surely we can too. Sometimes there is a fear when we are in the midst of our own creative process that if we stop, we won't be able to pick it back up and get back into the right frame of mind. Sometimes we get convinced that the moment of creating is magical, and we have to "seize the moment" and not let go when inspiration strikes.

While there are a lot of lessons to be concluded from God's choice to create with intentional moments of rest, perhaps one of the most important realities to consider is His confidence in the process. He knew He would see it through and wouldn't quit until it was done, no matter how many times He had to pick it back up. Therefore, resting was an allowable and welcome part of the process.

Rest isn't just about the sabbath, though. The spirit of rest should be carried throughout our day and really, every stage of the creative process. God reminded me of this recently through my daughter.

MAKE HIS FACE YOUR TARGET

I was vacuuming as my six and four-year-old played *quietly* in their room. (Clearly, God was already at work with His wonder-working power!) As a family, we were adjusting to the new norm of my husband working outside the home for the first time. Along with that new rhythm, I was also homeschooling, and writing my first book. My schedule was...*special*.

I was feeling frustrated at the tension of not having a clear plan for my day. I wanted to write, but I needed to vacuum. So there I was, muttering to myself my frustrations—part prayer, part complaint, part self-flagellation.

"Should I be writing right now? Cleaning is good too. What would I write about anyway? I don't have anything to say today. Maybe I won't have anything to say, ever...I should probably just stick to painting."

The negative self-talk concerning the creative process of writing was my cue to surrender to the Lord. I pay attention when my inner critic tries to throw me off course, slow me down, keep me small, and make me hate my work. So when *that* voice starts talking, my spirit is quick to rise up and turn to truth! I grabbed hold of those thoughts as best I could, and I laid them at the feet of Jesus.

I simply told Him the truth. *"God, I'm feeling like a failure today. I feel like I'm missing the mark because I'm vacuuming instead of writing, but I really want a clean house so I can feel more peaceful in order to write. If that's a sneaky excuse, show me, and help me to write today. And help me to be kind to myself."*

I didn't feel much better immediately, but I knew I had placed it in trustworthy hands, and He would speak eventually. As I finished vacuuming, I was feeling the physical, residual effects of anxiety. I sat on my bed, waiting for some sort of direction, and in walked my six-year-old daughter.

She handed me a folded piece of paper with writing on the outside. The writing on the outside said, "Guess 3 times," with the 3 written backwards. I gave three half-hearted guesses. *"Is it a picture of our family?"* This was her favorite picture to draw, so I thought I had it in the bag.

"No," she said sweetly with a grin. *"Two more guesses!"*

"A rainbow?" Her other favorite; I was pretty sure I got it that time.

"Nope!" She giggles, obviously taking delight in my wrong guesses. *"Last chance!"*

"OK. Not our family. Not a rainbow...a unicorn?"

"NO! Ha! It's a bullseye!" she exclaimed triumphantly.

I laughed as I opened it to see a yellow bullseye with red colored all around it. My mind quickly recalled a homeschool lesson we had done probably six months prior. In the lesson, we were memorizing Psalm 119:11, *"Your word I have hidden in my heart, that I might not sin against you."* She had asked what sin was, and so I drew a bullseye on the marker board and talked about "missing the mark." The exact phrase I had just said to God—in an instant, He had my full attention.

Then she excitedly proclaimed to me, *"It's yellow because it's the face of God. Yellow like His light. And the red all around the outside is because He said, "I'm taking care of the ashes."*

Woah! My six-year-old just mic-dropped a prophetic picture and then told me word-for-word what God was saying through it— *and I believed her.* I noticed an increase in His felt presence, so I asked Him what it meant.

"When you make My face your target, you can't miss. And I'm taking care of everything else because everything else is like ashes. It's passing away," He whispered.

I knew He was answering my weak prayer from earlier. The fear that I was "missing the mark" was suddenly stripped of its power as this yellow bullseye stared me in the face. My fear that I wasn't doing enough was just squashed. Suddenly, I had complete clarity—*all that is required is to seek His face.* That is the essence of true rest, and it can be done whether I'm vacuuming, writing, or in His word.

I love that a picture my six-year-old draws can carry the presence and word of the Lord. That simplicity is evidence to me that anointing doesn't come because of our effort or training. Anointing flows where the river has the least resistance. A child's heart is exactly that—open and free.

CREATING IN REST

One of the most powerful testimonies that has come from my artwork was of a painting that I gave little thought to. I was in a busy season and didn't have large chunks of time to paint. One day when passing by my studio, I noticed a pallet that had little balls of paint sitting on it from a few days prior. I knew from experience if I didn't pull back the dried skin on top and use the paint it would be dried and wasted by the next day.

I had about thirty minutes before my next commitment, so I grabbed a hexagon shaped canvas off my shelf that had been sitting overlooked for months. Originally, I bought it because I thought the shape was interesting, but I never went to it because I didn't know what to paint on it. That day I decided I would just use the drying paint so it didn't get wasted.

I smashed the canvas onto the remaining wet paint and quickly smeared it around giving little thought to it. I blended and pulled the paint far enough to cover the canvas and was satisfied that it had the possibility to become something down the road, but mostly I was just happy I didn't waste the paint by not using it!

Another afternoon, not too long after that, I had a similar small window of time and felt the urge to add to this tiny hexagon painting. Again, I reached for paint that would otherwise be wasted and just played. I did this three or four times, painting for fun in thirty-minute increments whenever the opportunity presented itself.

Eventually, I began to see what could be a landscape scene. I decided one afternoon to take a time-lapse of the rest of the painting, and mountains, trees, and a river emerged as I finished this unexpected piece.

I posted the video to my social media, and my friend, Hannah, commented that it resonated with her. A couple weeks later, I was headed to a women's retreat, and I knew Hannah was going to be my roommate. As I was about to leave the house, I heard the Holy Spirit remind me to grab the painting and gift it to her and to name it *Portal of Redemption.*

When I handed her the painting, God's presence dropped into the room. I'll let her tell the rest:

> "As soon as I saw this painting, I knew it had so much depth and was so interwoven with my personal life. It felt incredible to be connected this way to a painting. When Genavieve handed it to me and told me the name, I literally fell to the floor and began having encounters with the Lord. He brought me to so many places in my history with Him and also with my family. There has been a lot of brokenness within my family. As a widow raising my own kids, there is so much that I hope to see this side of Heaven, but it's incredibly hard to keep the hope for redemption. I am from the mountains and grew up in a river town. This picture is of my river and my mountains. The shape of the painting is the shape of the home my parents built together from the trees on their property. It is literally where I was brought "home" and is now my father's dining room. There was so much symbolism that no one could have ever created this without the hand of Father being in it. He took me back to my baptism, to encounters and promises I have never shared. Every time I look at it, I am reminded of His profound love for me, my family, my lineage, my history, my future, and I have the tangible hope of what Jesus paid for on the cross."
>
> — HANNAH RABIU

What I love about this testimony is that the entire painting was done in rest. There was zero striving or performance involved. I said *yes* to His quiet invitation to sit and paint—if only for a few minutes between tasks. I gave my yes, enjoyed the restful space and mindless play, and God moved.

I had no idea Hannah's childhood home was built in the shape of a hexagon! Or that the land that surrounded it looked like what I painted.

I love my friend and would have loved to take credit for knowing all those things, but the truth is I simply enjoyed the process of playing and following Holy Spirit's lead, and something powerful and anointed came out. My heart was open and free as I created, so He flowed through it easily!

THERE IS ONLY ONE WAY

There are no shortcuts in life—not for anything of lasting value anyway. When I became a parent, I had no idea how hard it would be. For me, it's not hard primarily because of the sleep loss, loud noises, or even the ridiculous amount of literal poop you have to deal with in the early years. Parenting is difficult because love is difficult—real love anyway, not the easy romantic love that puts you in a trance and floats you through life without a care in the world. That kind of love is easy.

Real love, sacrificial love, involves commitment and faithfulness, and saying *yes* even when you're so tired you literally can't see straight. It means getting on your face to seek God instead of yelling at the top of your lungs and apologizing sincerely when you mess up.

One day, when I was in the thick of early parenthood with a two-year-old and a six-month-old, I got out of bed to respond to a cry coming from the direction of their bedrooms. When I stood, the room moved, and when I stopped moving, my body and the room didn't stop moving. It felt like the bedroom floor had become a merry-go-round and the centrifugal force sent me to the ground.

Confusion gripped me for a second. Was I having a stroke? Why couldn't I see straight? The room was still spinning. For those reading who've experienced this phenomenon, you probably already know what was happening to me. I was experiencing vertigo for the first time.

After a frantic yell downstairs to my husband who was working from home and a video call with a virtual doctor, I learned that the flu I had just recently gotten over was likely causing this "temporary inconvenience" and that it would likely clear up "within a few weeks."

What?! A FEW weeks?!

I was completely incapacitated. There was no way I was going to make it through a few weeks of this funhouse shenanigan my inner ear was performing. When you are a full-time, at home caregiver, you don't get PTO.

I remember saying out loud, "I can't see straight! This is so frustrating!" as I would stubbornly push through my day, gripping walls and counters. Looking back, I'm shaking my head at myself. I should've slowed *way* down and honored my body that was trying to heal.

I also see that whole scenario as an accurate metaphor for what the first two to three years of parenting felt like for me. Life felt like a never-ending to-do list of other people's needs that often left me spinning. I wasn't responding to the beautiful season of life I was in, but rather I was constantly reacting to the perceived urgency of the needs around me. My life was like a riptide taking me out to sea, and I couldn't find the horizon anymore. I didn't choose rest, and so eventually, it chose me through my body crying out for it!

Babies don't care if you're tired. They don't care if you're overwhelmed and don't have it together. They don't care if you didn't find time to shower and are wearing the same oversized nursing shirt from yesterday. They don't care that you haven't had a stimulating adult conversation in months, and you literally feel like your brain is atrophying. They show no regard for your REM cycles, your unexplained weight gain, your hormonal imbalance, or your low sex-drive.

They just don't care. They aren't supposed to! But *you should.* You should care about yourself enough to make rest a priority—not just sleep, but rest that fills your cup to overflowing. You need the kind of rest that keeps the rivers inside your belly flowing with the creative life of God! Because that's the life Jesus died for you to have. That's the life the Creator wants to partner with you to create!

> *"Believe in me so that rivers of living water will burst out from within you, flowing from your innermost being, just like the Scripture says!"*
>
> — JOHN 7:38, TPT

He is The Way, beloved. He showed us what love looks like on the cross. Real love. No shortcuts. Bruised, exposed, holding nothing back —He was the passion of God our Creator on full display, suffering for us.

In order for Him to get the full reward of His suffering, you need to embrace and walk in your birthright as a co-creator. It doesn't matter your profession or your circumstance in life—your identity as an image bearer of the Creator is rooted in Him, developed with Him, and enjoyed *most* by Him.

Letting the creative, life-giving flow of His Spirit move through you in everything you do is the definition of the abundant life He died to give you. So choose rest, beloved. Choose it before it chooses you. Work it into your life intentionally to make room for more life!

CHAPTER SUMMARY

- God's rest isn't from something, it's to enjoy something. It's not passive. It's part of His process.
- Rest begets more life when done in the right spirit—the sabbath spirit.

- Daily, weekly, even yearly, sabbath rests should be worked into our lives to maintain the health of our hearts.
- Just like the land, our hearts need sabbath rests to be fertile and fully functional and to protect the creative flow of life that is meant to proceed from it.
- If God can rest, surely we can, too.
- The spirit of rest should be carried throughout our day, and really, every stage of the creative process.
- All that is required for sabbath rest is to seek His face.

QUESTIONS FOR REFLECTION

1. Is rest an intentional part of the flow of your life? Do you have daily, weekly, monthly, and yearly rests scheduled into your and your family's life?

2. When was the last time you felt deep, soul-reviving rest?

3. What does it mean to you that God rested? Ask Holy Spirit how He defines rest.

4. What would it look like for you to integrate rest into the rhythms of your life? What's something you could do daily to create an intentional space for rest?

CHAPTER 7

HOW THE CREATOR LOVES THE CREATIVE PROCESS OF RELATIONSHIP

"Who is this one? Look at her now! She arises out of the desert, clinging to her beloved. When I awakened you under the apple tree, as you were feasting upon me, I awakened your innermost being with the travail of birth as you longed for more of me."

— Song of Songs 8:5, TPT

Now, let's connect the dots. We've covered the Creator's Process in Genesis—so let's explore how that process aligns with the depiction of the process in the Song of the Songs of the preparation of the Bride for the Bridegroom. In this beautiful love story, we see the fingerprints of the Creator and His work in the midst of a Bridegroom conquering the heart of the woman He loves. It's a poignant allegory of the love God has for His creation. Moreover, it carries within its text a blueprint for our hearts to navigate the firestorm of loving God with our whole hearts.

OUR BRIDEGROOM GOD

God chose to reveal Himself to us throughout scripture as a bridegroom, which makes us (male and female) His bride. The unique and unwavering intimacy between a husband and wife (when done well of course) is a picture of the unveiled, vulnerable relationship He is calling us into. This kind of love is built over time with a million little choices. Choices to honor, respect, trust, forgive, and live with the covenant you've made in mind at all times.

He has already demonstrated His level of commitment to us with arms outstretched, fully exposed and laid bare on the cross. His invitation as a Bridegroom is an offering of deeper intimacy than that of sexual intimacy with a spouse. He has made a way for spirit-to-spirit relationship, dwelling inside of us, inviting us to partner with Him, forever.

In the same way that He says He is the Bread of Life and Living water, yet we do not *physically* eat or drink Him; the description of our relationship to Him as the Bride of Christ doesn't mean we'll *physically* marry Him. When we look to Him as the Bread of Life, we are acknowledging that He gives us spiritual sustenance greater than the physical sustenance bread offers. When we find Him as the living water, He is like a refreshing drink for our souls, the solution for our soul's thirst. When we find Him as our Bridegroom, He is the perfect match for our need for intimate communion with another—the need to be seen and known and to walk alongside someone. And the amazing gospel reality is that we have that desire because *He had it first.*

If understanding our identity as the Bride of Christ is so simple, why then is it often easier for us to understand Him in metaphorical terms as the Bread of Life rather than the Bridegroom? Perhaps the answer lies in our perceptions of God as the provider for the physical needs of survival more than the emotional needs of our soul? Perhaps we value the needs of our soul less, or perhaps we simply only have faith for the God of "just enough"? If we know Him primarily as Provider, then relating to Him as the generous lover of our soul is a leap not easily made.

I think it's easy to overthink the term Bridegroom in particular. Maybe because on some levels it seems too good to be true. Maybe we are scared to believe something our hearts long for on such a fundamental level—*personal, intimate depth of relationship with our Creator.*

But what if it's not too good to be true? What if He is in fact the very definition of goodness? Maybe we know more than we think about who God is. The universal experience of falling in love tells us so much about the human heart. Regardless of doctrine, culture, or life experience, we are all familiar with the notion of falling in love. Again, I believe our stories of love are deeply personal, but yet universal, and therefore we can learn so much from them.

When my husband Arin and I met, things happened fast. We met on a worship team that served at an inner city prayer room. When my car wouldn't start one morning, I asked for a ride to our set. That's when we found out we lived just a couple doors down from each other. Divine set-up? He began driving me to and from sets three times a week, and we often laughed the whole thirty minute drive. We were engaged just a few short months after that.

As is the case for so many dating stories, we quickly became infatuated, and it became difficult to fit anything else into our lives. We spent as much time as we could with each other, and talked and texted in between. Even in writing this, I am blushing, thinking about how hard I fell for him. I remember him coming over at 11:00 p.m. after he got off work just to say good night, which always turned into at least an hour of silly banter. Some nights we would just talk for hours and our conversation would carry us into the dawn. We had it bad!

The intoxicating reality of new love causes us to blissfully stumble through life for a season, giving little notice to any other peripheral issues. There is a reality in God that is similar in nature to this love-drunk stupor.

As His Bride, He declares over us that we have His full attention. He wants to take us into deep, vulnerable conversations that bend time and carry us into the dawn. He longs to fill our thoughts, to woo our hearts, to cause us to think differently (as if anything is possible), and to see the beauty and wonder in the world because He made it. He wants us to live unhindered, oozing love everywhere we go.

> *"Suddenly, he transported me into his house of wine—he looked upon me with his unrelenting love divine."*
>
> — SONG OF SONGS 2:4, TPT

In other translations, this verse says, *"His banner over me is love."* In the time that the *Song of Songs* was written, houses or tribes had banners that represented them. It was a symbol of belonging, destiny, and even prophetic utterance of that family. What God is saying in this verse is that we belong to the tribe of love. It is our family crest.

Love is our home—our destiny. It is the prophetic utterance over our lives. In His house of wine, we encounter the intoxicating reality of His unrelenting love. His never-ending, never giving-up love.

GOD, YOUR CREATOR, IS LOVE

To walk in your identity as the Bride of Christ under the tribal banner of "Love" is to choose vulnerability—because you can't have love without it. It means choosing to relate to Him from a place of authenticity. We have to come out from our hiding places, from behind ideas *about* Him, and open ourselves up to actually *encounter* Him.

Maybe you've been hurt deeply before, cut to the core by the wound of a love that was less than perfect. Maybe the notion of living in such an exposed manner in relationship with a person you can't even see causes you to feel insecure and uncomfortable. We have all been hurt before, but even if there is resistance to the notion of vulnerability, we inevitably open our hearts for deeper connection again.

It's as if some unseen force is leading us beyond our survival mode of self-protection. Our ability to love despite pain is evidence that we were made for more than mere survival. It is the very fingerprints of a selfless God revealed in our lives. He endured suffering in every form on the cross—physical, spiritual, emotional. It was both an act of perfect love and great suffering. If we are to be His partner, His Bride, we are called to love like that.

The bridal paradigm language isn't flowery prose for the romantics. It's a call to the battle of Love that the Kingdom of God is fighting. We are His Beloved, lovesick and surrendered to His ways. This isn't a position of weakness, but great strength in vulnerability.

When we discover the reality of our identity, which is a process we see through the Song of Songs, we are empowered to walk worthy of the title of "Beloved," to be the one He calls, *"My beloved, my equal, my bride."*[1] We are empowered to cast off the snares that so easily entangle,[2] to remove the foxes that eat the fruit in our vineyards.[3] We are empowered to run. And Run we must because our Beloved is leaping on the mountains, graceful as a gazelle. Free from everything that hinders love, our Bridegroom King is leading the way, and we must start by recognizing His call.

Assuming you have heard Him calling, and you have worked through any resistance, what then is next? What does it really look like to align yourself with Jesus? It is one thing to talk about the idea of Jesus as the Bridegroom wanting to run with His beloved; it is quite another to experience it in everyday life.

If we aren't careful, we can believe the idea of being loved so perfectly —wanted and invited into an adventure with God—but we can actually miss the tangible application of it to our lives. His invitation to *run on the mountains* isn't ethereal; it's actually very practical.

The mountains we are invited to run on with Jesus are part of the process of transforming our hearts into the garden paradise we read about in Genesis. God's desire has always been to dwell with us in unhindered intimacy. When Eden was closed to humans, God did not give up on His dream, or on us. In fact, He moved in closer and determined to make the very heart within us His new garden paradise. This glorious ideal doesn't come without cost though—Jesus gave His life for it, and ours is required, too. We must fellowship with Him in His sufferings through our own daily dying.[4]

Running with God in this way is a daily decision that involves your choices, your self-awareness, and your willingness to adjust when you find something that's out of alignment with His heart. Ultimately, your journey with God is the process of shedding the false identities that tell you you can't run like Him, that you can't love like Him. This process of maturing in love is not just the Shulamite's story—it's all our stories. The goal is the same, that we become one with the Beloved—His equal, His Bride—leaning on Him in voluntary surrender.

In an earthly marriage, if one partner was living in freedom, joy, and peace while the other was depressed, fearful, insecure, and subject to shame cycles, there would be some obvious roadblocks to their intimacy. It is no different in our relationship with Jesus. The good news is that He is fully committed to freeing us from all those roadblocks and bringing us into the freedom of surrender.

His commitment to us is as fierce as that which is displayed in the story of the Bridegroom-King and the Shulamite. Even when the Shulamite denies the Bridegroom King's first invitation to run on the mountains, his love does not waver. The same God who created the stars loves us with that kind of relentless pursuit. The same Master Artist who created the universe through His *creative process* wins and matures our heart through the *process of love*. The same pattern (of incubation, invitation, execution, evaluation and blessing, and rest) found in the creation account in Genesis can also be found in the

Song of Songs. If Genesis is a book of beginnings that tells *how* we came into existence, Song of Songs could be considered the book of *why* we came into existence.

If we have eyes to see, then God's creative process is evident throughout the love story of the Bridegroom King and the Shulamite. If this book shows us anything, it shows us clearly that God loves the process of maturing us in love. He is not bothered that it takes time to fully win our hearts. He is not shocked at our resistance, offended by our sin, or surprised when our love is hindered in a million different ways.

Without force, manipulation, or control God only asks for our *yes*. He doesn't focus on our shortcomings like we so often do. Instead, He simply receives our yes as love, knowing that everything else will get sorted out along the way. We are His masterpiece in the process of becoming what He's *already* predestined us to be, and He is delighted to help us discover who that is.

THE CREATOR'S HEART

The Bible provides a framework for understanding life. It tells us who we are and helps us understand the mysteries of life. But the greatest treasure of all is that it reveals to us the heart of our Creator.

Taking the whole of the Bible into view, Genesis reveals we were formed from the dust, and the book of Revelation reveals we are becoming the Bride of Christ, equally yoked and full of the Holy Spirit. So how does dust become something so glorious? The plain and simple answer is perfect love. Song of Songs, found right in the middle of the Bible, is the key that unlocks the transformation process through which we mature from the dust to the Bride.

The Shulamite's journey from shepherdess to a perfectly matched partner for the King is a kind of allegory that depicts all of our journeys. Let's take a quick glance at the Creator's process of maturing our love as displayed in the Song of Songs.

BROODING:

"Let him smother me with kisses—his Spirit-kiss divine. So kind are your caresses, I drink them in like the sweetest wine! Your presence releases a fragrance so pleasing—over and over poured out. For your lovely name is "Flowing Oil." No wonder the brides-to-be adore you."

— Song of Songs 1:2-3, TPT

The story starts with a picture of the secret place. It's thick with presence and love exchange. The remainder of Chapter 1 reveals the wrestle in the secret place for the Shulamite's identity. She loves him, but she does not yet love herself as he loves her. The budding signs of transformation are evident in chapter two as she begins to lean into grace.

"My beloved is to me the most fragrant apple tree—he stands above the sons of men. Sitting under his grace-shadow, I blossom in His shade, enjoying the sweet taste of his pleasant, delicious fruit, resting with delight where his glory never fades."

— Song of Songs 2:3, TPT

INVITATION:

"Can you not discern this new day of destiny breaking forth around you? The early signs of my purposes and plans are bursting forth. The budding vines of new life are now blooming everywhere. The fragrance of their flowers whispers, "There is change in the air." Arise, my love, my beautiful companion, and run with me to the higher place. For now is the time to arise and come away with me."

— Song of Songs 2:13, TPT

What an incredible invitation! He is vulnerable and freely expressing his love for her in the verses leading up to this invitation. He isn't blind to the maturing process she is in though. Therefore, he issues a request with his invitation in verse 15:

"You must catch the troubling foxes, those sly little foxes that hinder our relationship. For they raid our budding vineyard of love to ruin what I've planted within you. Will you catch them and remove them for me? We will do it together."

— SONG OF SONGS 2:15, TPT.

When he invites her to come away with him, he sees the sly little foxes of fear and self-doubt still holding her back from the fullness of the life she could be living with him. In His kindness, he tells her the truth. Jesus always tells us the truth. He never condemns, but He will not wink at sin or ignore a fox that is destroying your vineyard.

I love that He extends invitations to us even when He knows we will likely say no. God in His kindness will invite us into things we are not prepared for, giving us the opportunity to leap into the unknown through faith. He is *so* confident in the perfecting power of His love that He knows even if we decline the invitation, He can use it for our good. Sadly, the Shulamite does decline his first invitation into the unknown and clearly states her reasons.

"I know my lover is mine and I have everything in you, for we delight ourselves in each other. But until the day springs to life and the shifting shadows of fear disappear, turn around, my lover, and ascend to the holy mountains of separation without me. Until the new day fully dawns, run on ahead like the graceful gazelle and skip like the young stag over the mountains of separation. Go on ahead to the mountain of spices—I'll come away another time."

— SONG OF SONGS 2:16-17, TPT

This denial offers us valuable insight. When she says no to the execution stage of running with him on the mountains, she enters right back into *brooding*, but this time he's not there. She wrestles with her soul—sleepless, angsty, and longing for His nearness again. She gets wounded by leaders who don't understand her season, and she searches tirelessly for Him.

Though it's not ideal, his absence is being used to stoke the fires in her heart. It moves her out of entitlement and grows her into a newfound appreciation for her Bridegroom. Her desire to be with him begins to override her fears of the unknown.

After she cries out for him to come back to her, he returns.

Beloved, if you are in a season of longing for more of Him, don't stop knocking. He will come!

In chapter 4 the Bridegroom comes back and declares his love for the Shulamite again. This time he notices the change that has occurred in her. The refining fire of perfect love has matured her. This is one of the things he says to her:

> *"When I look at you, I see how you have taken my fruit and tasted my word. Your life has become clean and pure, like a lamb washed and newly shorn. You now show grace and balance with truth on display."*
>
> — SONG OF SONGS 4:2, TPT

The shulamite's growth is the direct result of doing the hard work of catching and removing foxes from her vineyard. It is the hard work of giving up wrong thinking and aligning her heart and mind with His.

The result of this growth is a brave heart. She declares that she has changed her mind and is no longer held back by fear.

> *"I've made up my mind. Until the darkness disappears and the dawn has fully come, in spite of shadows and fears, I will go to the mountaintop with you—*

the mountain of suffering love and the hill of burning incense. Yes, I will be
your bride."

— SONG OF SONGS 4:6, TPT

Her *yes* moves the Shulamite into a new experience—*the execution*
stage.

EXECUTION:

"Come, all my friends—feast upon my bride, all you revelers of my palace.
Feast on her, my lovers! Drink and drink, and drink again, until you can take
no more. Drink the wine of her love. Take all you desire, you priests. My life
within her will become your feast."

— SONG OF SONGS 5:1B, TPT

The Shulamite and Bridegroom go back and forth declaring and
enjoying their love. Their love exchange opens up and others are
somehow able to partake. This dynamic is a picture of our relationship with Jesus becoming a life-giving force that ministers to others.
No matter what we are doing, the heart of the execution stage is
allowing Jesus and His Kingdom to be known and experienced by
others!

EVALUATION:

"After this I let my devotion slumber, but my heart for him stayed awake."

— SONG OF SONGS 5:2A, TPT

At this point, the Shulamite evaluates the state of her heart and
describes a dream she has in the night. In the dream, the Bridegroom
comes and asks for more of her heart. She isn't sure how she can give

more because she feels she has already given so much. I can't help but wonder if this is a picture of spiritual burnout.

Sometimes, when we are *doing* with God, we forget the purpose of the brooding stage. We become Marthas.[5] I suspect this is what the shulamite was feeling because I know from experience when we are trapped in *doing,* we can forget to take care of ourselves. When that happens, the request from Jesus for more of our heart can feel like another task. That's when we know our devotion has grown cold and the fires of love need tending so that they can blaze brightly once again.

After this evaluation, there seems to be a jump back into the brooding, then more invitations, execution, and evaluation as the Shulamite is refined. Her love grows deeper and deeper as she aligns with His heart. She learns to love herself as he loves her. She learns to let his love define her. She is no longer looking within herself for the strength or ability to execute anything. She eventually declares that love has made her a tower of passion and contentment.[6] Once the process has brought about perfect love, they enter into rest.

REST:

> *"His left hand cradles my head while his right hand holds me close. We are at rest in this love."*

> — Song of Songs 8:3, TPT

Then from the Bridegroom's perspective:

> *"Who is this one? Look at her now! She arises out of her desert, clinging to her beloved. When I awakened you under the apple tree, as you were feasting upon me."*

> — Song of Songs 8:5, TPT

If the Song of Songs is a sketch of the maturing process we all must go through, then we can make a few conclusions about that process that are important for our lives. First of all, we see that becoming the bride is a process. Saying one prayer doesn't necessarily mean that your heart is fully surrendered. It's important, but it's only the beginning.

Secondly, God is really confident in His love for us and His ability to lead us into maturity. If He doesn't offer a way to circumvent the process, we shouldn't be looking for one.

Lastly, God is always looking for voluntary lovers. You always have a choice. Just like in marriage, intimacy would be hindered if one or both partners didn't feel they had the freedom to say no to the other. The moments, or even seasons, of our stories where we have said no to Jesus don't need to be our shame. He can use all things for our good if we allow Him to!

CHAPTER SUMMARY

- Song of Songs is a blueprint for the process God takes us through to win our hearts fully.
- God chose to reveal Himself as a Bridegroom for a reason. He wants covenant.
- He is fully committed to helping us to be free from all the sly little foxes.
- Genesis is a book of beginnings that tells us *how* we came into existence; Song of Songs tells us *why*.
- His tribal banner over you is love. You belong to the tribe of love.
- His invitation to "run on the mountains" isn't ethereal. It's lived out *practically* through your choices.
- We can't become God's equally-yoked bride if we are bogged down by fear.

QUESTIONS FOR REFLECTION

1. Have you ever given Jesus a "no"? Talk to Holy Spirit about it, and write down what you hear Him saying.

2. Do you evaluate yourself the way God does? Ask Holy Spirit to show you any thoughts you've had recently about yourself that He doesn't agree with.

3. If you had to compare your current season to a particular point in the Shulamite's journey, where would you be?

4. What does "leaning on your beloved" mean to you?

---

1. Song of Songs 4:9, TPT "For you reach into **my** heart. With one flash of your eyes I am undone by your love, **my** beloved, **my equal**, **my** bride. You leave me breathless — I am overcome by merely a glance from your worshiping eyes, for you have stolen **my** heart. I am held hostage by your love and by the graces of righteousness shining upon you."
2. See Hebrews 12:1, TPT.
3. See Song of Songs 2:15, TPT.
4. See SS 4:16-5:1, TPT; SS 4:6, TPT; and Matthew 16:24, TPT.
5. See Luke 10:41-42, TPT.
6. See Song of Songs 8:10, TPT

PART II
SLY LITTLE FOXES

CHAPTER 8

THE NATURE OF A FOX

"You must catch the troubling foxes, those sly little foxes that hinder our relationship. For they raid our budding vineyard of love to ruin what I've planted within you. Will you catch them and remove them for me? We will do it together."

— Song of Songs 2:15, TPT

In the transforming process of maturing love, the Shulamite in the Song of Songs has to confront the foxes that seek to ruin her love with the Bridegroom King. Those foxes are what caused her to decline his first invitation to run on the mountains. It was a process of removing those foxes that empowered her to say yes to her Bridegroom at the second invitation to run with him.

I relate deeply to this story. Saved at fourteen years old, I loved Jesus genuinely and the best I could until the foxes became an issue. I found myself saying no to Jesus for the first time despite my love for Him. He brought me through a process of learning to recognize and name those foxes which enabled me to run with Him in a new way. It's that part of my story, learning to remove the foxes, where I became utterly convinced of His love and His ability to transform.

In Part II, I want to talk about the nitty gritty of God's process in our lives. It's the application portion, so get your pen and journal ready. I'm going to share some of my stories and the lessons I've learned while catching my most troublesome foxes —shame, fear, comparison, and rejection.

HIS EYES OF LOVE

In the summer of 2008, I packed up my entire life into a gold Saturn Ion and moved across the country to Kansas City at the Lord's leading. I was going to be a part of the International House of Prayer, and I was excited about all the new unlived life that was ahead of me.

It may sound like a pretty straightforward story of a girl in her early twenties on a spiritual journey, but the path to that moment involved one of the biggest and darkest pits of my life that only God could have gotten me out of, and He did! It is the part of my story that can be difficult for me to talk about, but I'm choosing to share with you, dear reader, because the Jesus I met in that pit is too glorious not to share.

On the day He rescued me out of that pit, everything changed for me. It was a pivotal moment in my story upon which the next beautiful decades came from. God orchestrated a series of events and graciously removed the veil from my mind to see a dating relationship I was in for what it was, and the compromises I was making to be in it.

That relationship was the bad fruit of the pit I had dug for myself, one choice at a time—and I had lots of foxes to help. I was like the proverbial frog that gets boiled by slowly increasing the temperature of the water. If I had known at the beginning of the relationship how much I would betray myself and all my promises to Jesus along the way, I wouldn't have started it. But compromise doesn't play fair. It doesn't tell you what it'll take from you. It just offers the immediate gratification of the thing you think you want.

When I say the veil was removed, that sounds spiritual and gentle, light and airy. This was more like ripping a bandaid off an infected wound. Visceral and raw. It felt like my flesh was torn and festering and exposed.

I won't go into all the details, but I'll just say it happened quickly, in a matter of moments. In the time it took for me to walk from my car to my second-floor apartment, my life completely changed gears, like a car flying down the highway that's suddenly thrown into park. It was one of those heart traumas that knocks the wind out of you and completely reorients everything.

I remember putting my keys in the lock of my apartment and feeling like I was going to pass out. My vision was tunneled, my ears were ringing, my cheeks were flushed and wet from tears I didn't even realize I was crying. I was being confronted with the state of my vineyard, and it was not pretty. I unconsciously moved through the motions of getting myself in the shower, which I see now as a profound metaphor for what was happening in the spirit without my awareness.

I crumpled to my knees on the cold hard porcelain tub. Sobs erupting from my deepest places. The ache was so intensely paralyzing. Jesus was my everything for nearly ten years up to that season, and I had said no to Him, walked away, hurt my Beloved. There was no longer anywhere to hide from that glaring, soul-crushing truth.

I was spinning. Where could I go? Who could help me in such a state? I assumed God was as disappointed and disgusted with me as I was. "God help," was all I could muster out through sobs.

Suddenly, I saw Him in my mind's eye clearer than I ever had until then. He was looking right at me with His hand extended. His eyes were focused and resolute. I saw pain in His eyes, but not pain directed at me, pain *for* me—this was deeply personal to Him. The image was so clear and transcendent, almost as if I were somewhere else, unaware of the cold shower floor and hot running water on my back. I experienced nothing in that moment but Him.

His eyes communicated His heart, and my spirit knew Him in that moment. I saw fire in His eyes—not literal fire, not angry fire, just a heart-exposing presence that burned away everything that didn't matter. He was passionate and direct, looking into me. I looked back. I let Him see me—in all my pain and confusion and utter weakness—I let Him see me.

In a long moment of silent eye contact I couldn't find any words to justify, explain, or even to ask for forgiveness. I never wanted to hurt this One. I never wanted to break a promise to Him or cause His heart pain, but I knew I had. I could see it because He wasn't hiding it, and neither was I.

Even though there was pain there, I sensed no accusation in Him. I felt safe as well as vulnerable. Extremely vulnerable. More exposed and seen then I had ever been...but safe.

Without breaking His intense gaze, He calmly, with full authority and perfect love, said, "We are going to pick up where we left off." With those words, He spoke to the storm in my heart and it was instantly silenced. Peace. No more crashing waves. No more loud thunder. Just His eyes, and peace.

I saw myself put my hand in His, and just like that, I was back in the present moment, shower still running, beating down on my back. I stood up slowly. "Did that really happen?" I silently wondered as my mind tried to make sense of the event. I turned off the shower and slowly moved in a daze to my room and found my journal. I wrote the words He spoke to me and wondered at them.

"We are going to pick up where we left off."

I suddenly *knew* things as those words unpacked themselves onto the pages of my journal. My hand wrote furiously as I prophesied to myself what would come next. I knew one of the things He meant in that statement was that I was going to move to Kansas City. Earlier, at the beginning of the year, He had told me I would move to KC when my lease was up in June. It was now May, and I hadn't made any progress.

I asked Him some questions, and told Him I needed a place to live, a job, and money to move—none of which I had any clue how to attain. Soon after that day, I reconnected with one of my friends from a prayer group I had been a part of prior to the season of compromise. I came to find out that, even though I was avoiding their calls and being a terrible friend, they were fasting and praying for me the whole time! I am so thankful for their prayers!

I told her nervously what God said, scared she would laugh and think I was arrogant for assuming God would just "pick up where we left off." She smiled with tears in her eyes and began to tell me her story of heartbreaking compromise that she had walked through a few years prior. Then she remembered a prayer missionary she supported in Kansas City that was a house manager. One phone call later, and I had a room secured within walking distance to the prayer room.

Shortly after that, I received a card in the mail from a friend I hadn't seen in a year or so. In it, he wrote the kindest words of encourage-ment and life, having no idea what I was walking out of. He thanked me for the ways my friendship had "ministered" to him over the years and said he felt led to tithe off an inheritance he'd received to sow into my "ministry." Tears rolled down my cheeks as I opened the check for $3000! God was doing it. He was making the way, and we really were going to pick up where we left off.

Next, I was at work, and I heard the Lord's whisper. I was a shift manager at Starbucks, and I heard Him say to look up stores in KC and start calling and asking if they needed a shift manager. The first store I called told me they just had a shift manager give their notice!

"Can you be here in three weeks?" the manager joked.

"YES!" I said. That was exactly when my lease was ending!

And just like that, we had picked up where we left off, and I moved to Kansas City with a job, a room to rent, and money to get me started. For what exactly I wasn't sure, but I knew I was following the Lord's leading, and I couldn't have been happier about that. Just like the Shulamite in Song of Songs 3:4, "...I encountered him. I found the One I adore! I caught him and fastened myself to him, refusing to be feeble in my heart again..."

I had pain and confusion in my heart over my ability to love Him and yet to have said no to Him. I found solace in trusting in His love for me, rather than the other way around. I spent the first few months of my time in my new home working the opening shift at the coffee shop and then spending the rest of my day crying in the prayer room in God's presence.

I didn't know what was next; I just knew I wasn't letting go of Him ever again. My confidence had shifted from the strength of my love, to the strength of His, and He was about to teach me how to catch some foxes!

THE WAY THROUGH

In the first months in my new home, I went slow. I wasn't interested in moving quickly toward anything. I just wanted to be with Him. Eventually I caught the excitement of the idea of going through the school of ministry and picked up an application. It took me a month to fill it out, and even after I was done, I just didn't have peace that I was supposed to turn it in.

After some time of seeking, I thought maybe an internship was the structure I needed and got an application for that. Again, after a month of sitting on it, I just decided I didn't have peace. I was beginning to think I was just going to work at my coffee shop and sit in the prayer room for the rest of my life. And to be honest, I was ok with that because I was deeply connected to God's presence in my life.

Shortly after filling out the second application that I never turned in, I saw an announcement in the Sunday service bulletin. It was for a six month inner healing course that focused on same and opposite sex relational dynamics. It was like a spotlight was shining down on it. I felt the Lord's nudge, and I knew. This is what was next.

Someone got up to make an announcement about the course. They made it sound really heavy and intense so as to weed out those who might not see it through. They said things like: "You might cry everyday." "Emotional and relational healing isn't an easy path." "This isn't for the faint of heart." And, "Make sure this is what God is telling you to do before you commit." For some reason this made me want to do it all the more.

And they weren't wrong.

For six months, I went through a six inch workbook, met weekly with a small group of women going after the same things, told my most painful stories of my parents divorce, childhood abuse from peers, and sexual sin.

Christians talk about sin in generalities in the church, but we don't like to get specific. Granted, there is a time and place for those conversations, but I will say shame gets broken when sin is brought into the light. Learning to recognize and expose the cycles of shame in your life is deeply liberating to those seeking healing. I heard complete strangers tell their stories with more courage and holy vulnerability than I'd ever experienced—and I cried. Everyday.

It was a season of my foundation getting reworked. God showed me how I had built my house with Him on a faulty foundation of false identity and an immature understanding of Him. Abuse, abandonment, and lies, sown in my heart at an early age, had created an entire ecosystem of twisted realities that felt normal. The painful disconnect I felt as well as the confusion over my choices that didn't align with my genuine love for Him were because there was a giant crack in my foundation, and there were all manner of "foxes" living in there.

That season was hard. I expected that, but I didn't know how hard it would be. I thought that the first encounter I had with Him in the shower, when He calmed the raging storm in my heart in a moment, was it. I was secretly hoping that single encounter had somehow fixed everything, but it hadn't. That moment was sacred, and it put me back on the path with Him—but walking the path required my participation—my *yes*—step by step and yes by yes.

I was determined to walk this path with Jesus. It was clearer than it had ever been to me that there was no way around this mountain. I was given a holy invitation to walk this path of suffering love, and in so doing, Jesus repaired my foundation.[1]

I shared this story with my church one Sunday, and afterward a friend shared with me a vision she had while I spoke. She said she saw the foundation of a house with a crack in the middle, and Jesus laid His cross in it, filling it completely. I love that picture!

One of my favorite quotes from Mike Bickle of the International House of Prayer is this, "You *can't* do God's part, and He *won't* do yours." This statement sums up the dynamic of catching the sly little foxes and maturing in love.

In Song of Songs 2:15, just before the Shulamite says no to the Bridegroom King's invitation, he says to her, *"You must catch the troubling foxes, those sly little foxes that hinder our relationship. For they raid our budding vineyard of love to ruin what I've planted within you. Will you catch them and remove them for me? We will do it together."*

Two things stand out to me here. He asks *her* to catch them. Then he says, *"We will do it together."* Could Jesus snap His fingers and rid our vineyards of the foxes? Yes. Will He? No.

There were more than a few times that I asked Him to just do it. *Just heal me already. Just make it better.* His response to me time and time again was, *I am with you.* I had to give my yes, and He promised to be with me. That's it. The only requirement for you to truly be in partnership with your Creator is your yes. Everything else is Him. Everything else is grace.

Beloved, if you are standing at the base of your mountain of suffering love, and the elevation seems daunting, take courage in knowing that the God of the universe, the One who dreamed you up, believes in you. In fact, He honors you *so* much that He gives you a choice.

He gave you free will and won't violate that. He honors your boundaries as an autonomous, intelligent being because He believes in you even more than you do. He knows who you are in your essence—truly free, able to run unhindered as an equally-yoked partner—*and He is enthralled with your beauty!*[2]

If you feel a stirring in your heart as you read this part of the book, like a sudden discomfort, God may want to process with you through some "foxes" in your vineyard. I encourage you to sit with the Lord as you go through the questions at the end of the chapter and let the Holy Spirit minister to you. He wants you to choose Him because you want Him, not because you think you should and not because you're scared of what will happen if you don't.

He wants to be known and seen and loved just like we do, so He gives us the gift of process so we have something to offer Him—*our yes!* The Creator gives us the process of perfect love. Mature love. Suffering love. What an incredible gift!

SOME PROPHETIC THOUGHTS ON FOXES

I felt led to google the nature of foxes since I don't really know much about them, and I came across some interesting facts that stood out to me.

They seemed almost prophetic in nature when I think about the things I experienced when catching and removing foxes from my own proverbial vineyard.

1. Foxes are common. They live on every continent except Antarctica and thrive in any environment from rural to urban. Despite that, they are elusive and mysterious.

Everyone has foxes in their vineyards. If you know Jesus, then you have fruit. If you've got fruit, you've got foxes. Sometimes we are shocked and ashamed when we ask the Lord to help us grow and tend to the vineyards and find way more foxes lurking in the shadows than we expected. However, shame is not your friend. In fact, it's a fox! God is not surprised by anything in your vineyard, so you don't need to be either. Tending to your vineyard is a lifelong process. The longer you are engaged in the process, the easier it is to recognize the fox tracks and find the hidden burrows. They might always be present, but catching and removing them gets easier with time and practice.

2. Foxes are solitary animals. While they might spend some time in small groups, called leashes, when they are raising their young, they live mostly solitary lives. They are survivalists by nature.

These foxes are sly, and they will do anything not to give up their homes and sources of food. Oftentimes, when we are in an intense season of inner-healing, we will discover rationalizations and story-lines we've believed our whole lives that are helping these foxes to stick around.

For example, when we've been victimized, self-protection seems rational. When we have lived out a cycle of sinful behavior despite our best efforts, shame seems reasonable. When we start poking around in those dens, there is a resistance that feels like us, but it's not us. That resistance is a sly fox dressed up like you. It's eating the fruit given to you by Jesus and hindering your relationship with Him.

3. Though they are related to wolves and jackals, foxes are very cat-like. They hunt at night, have vertically oriented pupils and walk on their toes, making them difficult to track.

How do you catch something that comes out mainly at night, is hard to track, and seems to have better survival skills than you? Thankfully, you have the Holy Spirit to help you. He knows you perfectly, has no falsehood in Him, and understands the nature of the human heart because He made it. This is why doing fox-catching with Him is so important. He gives us understanding and perspective that we just can't attain without Him. You can't *reason* a fox into a trap. You need supernatural power from Holy Spirit.

> **4.** Scientists theorize that foxes use the earth's magnetic field to hunt prey.[3] Visually they see a "ring of shadow" that darkens as they head true north. When the sound of their prey lines up with that shadow, they pounce. When they are pouncing from the northeast, they are more likely to pounce accurately and catch their prey.

When we are catching these foxes and removing them, it's deliverance. Plain and simple. There is a whole system of darkness at play here, and its tactics and ways of operating aren't fully known, but that's okay. You aren't supposed to understand them! You are a child of the light![4]

It might feel at times like you're getting pounced on, but you and Holy Spirit are an unstoppable team! This process is one of tearing down strongholds and changing thought patterns. In the natural, it's called neuroplasticity, which is your brain's ability to create new neural pathways. The older we get, the harder it is to change our neural map, but it's not impossible—it just takes time, repetition, and a supportive environment.[5]

Studies even show that learning a new skill—like a new language, a musical instrument, or even painting—can help our brains become more moldable and therefore make changing those thought patterns and behaviors easier![6] Those creative outlets can become a weapon in your hand when you are fox hunting!

DON'T BE SCARED OF A MESSY VINEYARD

As I sit here writing, I'm thinking about where you might be on your journey with the Creator, and how I can be most helpful to you. If this is all new to you, I want to say to you that this is a divine invitation—just like those divine invitations to transition from one phase of the creative process to another. Moving into an intentional season of inner-healing is a lot like attending to a neglected vineyard. There are vines to be pruned, weeds to be pulled, rocks to be removed, and soil to be fertilized and cultivated over time. And there are foxes and aphids and grub worms and grasshoppers.

Any gardener (or parent) can tell you that caring for living things requires ongoing attention and that it transpires in seasons. This isn't an invitation to a one time event. It's an invitation to a way of life, a way of being with Him.

If you feel like He's inviting you into an intentional season of cleaning up the vineyard, get some help. Don't go it alone. I am so incredibly thankful to the sisters and brothers who have walked with me in the midst of my healing.[7]

To those of you who resonate with these words because you've lived them in your own way, I want to say to you, "Keep going." Don't ever grow complacent in your devotion. Check in with Holy Spirit again today, and ask Him if there are any hidden fox burrows that have gone unseen.

Just like a marriage, our relationship with God takes intentionality. It takes consistency over time. It requires maintenance. Don't ever be afraid to "check-in" with God and ask Him to search your vineyard. That vineyard is the place of intimacy for you and Him. It's meant to be thriving and verdant—full of life! Be jealous for its upkeep and vitality!

If you've been feeling stagnant, stuck, or wishing life with God was as exciting as it was at the beginning, I've got great news—*what's ahead for you is greater glory!*[8] Your history with Him has only made the soil richer and the roots deeper. A little attention can go a long way in an established vineyard. And as you know, you can trust Him to lead you perfectly through this process.

———

I WANT to pray for you before you move on:

Father, thank You for every heart that will read these words. Thank You that they are Your precious vineyard, a place of rest and intimacy that You long to inhabit fully. Thank You for the process You have them in and that they can trust Your capable, gentle, and strong hands to carry them. They can trust Your eyes, full of light and love, to lead them. I ask You to provide a safe place with other brothers and sisters where they can share what You are doing in their hearts. I ask for prophetic sign-posts to encourage them along the way as they catch those sly foxes and, with Your help, remove them. Thank You for grace, endurance, and wisdom in the process. Thank You that their surrendered will plus You is a powerful combination, and together, You can handle anything that might come up in this process! In Jesus' name, I pray. Amen.

QUESTIONS FOR REFLECTION

1. Close your eyes, and using the eyes of your spirit (like we did in the imagination realm exercise) ask Holy Spirit to show you the current state of your vineyard? Just take a minute to settle in until you feel His presence increase. What do you see? What do you hear? What do you smell? What do you feel? Write down what He shows you.

2. Ask the Holy Spirit if there are any foxes hiding out in your vineyard. Write down whatever He shows you.

3. If you are feeling a divine invitation into a season of fox catching, ask the Holy Spirit for a safe friend to pray with along the way. Inviting people into our process is important and powerful. The more transparent and vulnerable you can be, the better. A lot of these foxes hate the light and will flee as soon as you acknowledge them out loud through prayer and confession.

4. Meditate on the Bridegroom King's words paraphrased from Song of Songs 6. Insert your name in the blanks, read it aloud, and then write down your heart's response back to Him.

> *O my beloved _____, you are lovely.*
> *When I see you in your beauty,*
> *I see a radiant city where we will dwell as one.*

> *You _____ are more pleasing than any pleasure,*
> *more delightful than any delight,*
> *you have ravished my heart,*
> *stealing away my strength to resist you.*

> *Even hosts of angels stand in awe of you _____.*
> *Turn your eyes from me; I can't take it anymore!*
> *I can't resist the passion of your eyes that I adore.*
> *Overpowered by a glance, my ravished heart—undone.*

> *Held captive by your love _____,*
> *I am truly overcome!*
> *The shining of your spirit _____*
> *shows how you have taken my truth*
> *to become balanced and complete.*

*Your beautiful blushing cheeks
reveal how real your passion is for me,
even hidden behind your veil of humility.*

*I could have chosen anyone,
but I have chosen you _____
You are unrivaled in beauty,
without equal, beyond compare,
the perfect one, the favorite one.*

---

1. Song of Songs 4:6, TPT "I've made up my mind. Until the darkness disappears and the dawn has fully come, in spite of shadows and fears, I will go to the mountaintop with you—the mountain of suffering love and the hill of burning incense." TPT footnote for "mountain of suffering love" reads, "Literally "the mountain of myrrh —the emblem of suffering love. To become the bride, she must experience Calvary, as did her Lord. We must be His co-crucified partner who will embrace the fellowship of his sufferings. See Gal 2:20 and Phil. 3:10.
2. "For your royal Bridegroom is ravished by your beautiful brightness. Bow in reverence before him, for He is your Lord!" Psalm 45:11 TPT "Turn your eyes from me; I can't take it anymore! I can't resist the passion of these eyes that I adore. Overpowered by a glance, my ravished heart—undone. Held captive by your love, I am truly overcome! For your undying devotion to me is the most yielded sacrifice." SOS 6:5 TPT
3. Marshall, Michael. "Foxes Zero in on Prey via Earth's Magnetic Field." New Scientist. New Scientist, January 12, 2011. https://www.newscientist.com/article/dn19945-foxes-zero-in-on-prey-via-earths-magnetic-field/?ignored=irrelevant#.VE7HBVNBH0o.
4. "Once your life was full of sin's darkness, but now you have the very light of our Lord shining through you because of your union with him. Your mission is to live as children flooded with his revelation-light!" Eph 5:8 TPT
5. Giang, Vivian. "What It Takes to Change Your Brain's Patterns after Age 25." Fast Company. Fast Company, April 30, 2015. https://www.fastcompany.com/3045424/what-it-takes-to-change-your-brains-patterns-after-age-25.
6. "What Is Neuroplasticity? A Psychologist Explains [+14 Exercises]." PositivePsychology.com, February 5, 2021. https://positivepsychology.com/neuroplasticity/.
7. If you don't have a pastor or inner healing ministry at your home church, www.bethelsozo.com is a powerful and safe ministry to reach out too. Having people in your daily life that you have relationship and accountability with is the ideal, but if you don't have that don't let it stop you!
8. *"We can all draw close to him with the veil removed from our faces. And with no veil we all become like mirrors who brightly reflect the glory of the Lord Jesus. We are being transfigured into his very image as we move from one brighter level of glory to another. And this glorious transfiguration comes from the Lord, who is the Spirit."* 1 Corinthians 3:18 TPT

CHAPTER 9

THE FOX CALLED SHAME

"Because you received a double dose of shame and dishonor, you will inherit a double portion of endless joy and everlasting bliss!"

— Isaiah 61:7, TPT

Jesus hates shame. Let's just start with that. He will fiercely and relentlessly wage war against shame in your life if you are willing to embrace the process. We tend to get uncomfortable when the topic of shame is brought up. Most people struggle to know how to talk about their shame or how to respond when someone else does. Not Jesus. He doesn't even flinch when someone exposes the shame they carry. In my experience, He looks you right in the eye.

Shame tells us there is something fundamentally wrong with us and causes us to hide who we are, to look away, or only share ourselves in guarded measure. When we choose to get real with Jesus about the presence of shame in our lives, we will find Him waiting with kind, soft eyes and an open heart. For He is not surprised by our immaturity, and He loves to tell us the truth about who we are!

Using the imagination realm exercise we did in chapter two can be a powerful tool for simply connecting with His gaze. Practicing looking into Jesus' eyes with the eyes of our spirit in the secret place creates a pathway in the spirit as well as a neurological pathway in our brain that enables us to do quick check-ins with Him when shame tries to hijack our identity and run the show.

A healthy child, when given freedom to run and play at a park, will check-in periodically to see if their caregiver is watching them. Their gaze is their safety-net, as it were, that allows them to run free. Likewise, if we practice locking eyes with Jesus in the secret place, we can more easily access His gaze when we are out in the world and in need of security or bravery.

The big world out there can be a treacherous place to navigate without an anchor or a compass. His eyes are both of those things. The Bible says that *"the eyes of your spirit allow revelation-light to enter your being. If your heart is unclouded, the light floods in!"*[1]

Nothing clouds our heart like shame, and those clouds block the light. If you have trouble holding people's gaze, especially Jesus' gaze, then you know shame is at play.

There is a biological significance and value behind eye contact that scientists have been studying for decades. A study done with newborns that were just two to five days old showed a clear difference in brain activity when given direct eye contact or an averted gaze.[2] As the infants get older, this exchange only grows in complexity. From the very beginning of our existence, we exchange information through eye contact. It seems our very existence is somehow subconsciously linked to eye contact.

Have you ever witnessed a three-year-old close their eyes when they are trying to hide from something? They aren't just being cute. A group of British scientists concluded after a series of experiments that even though they know their bodies can be seen, they differentiate a part of themselves that is rendered invisible when eye contact is hindered.[3]

What does any of this have to do with shame, you might be wondering. Everything. Shame is the cunning fox that convinces us there is something wrong with us, that we are somehow different from the others. Defective. Wrong. You can be sure that the fox called shame is lurking in your vineyard if a simple act of eye contact makes you squirm, and the thought of exposure makes your heart race.

When we feel shame, one of the tell-tale signs is a change in eye contact. I like to think of my relationship with Jesus as a form of eye contact. The eyes of my spirit and His eyes are locked, and I know something is amiss when I can't find His gaze, don't want to give Him mine, or I'm too busy to bother.

I often think… No, scratch that… God often *reminds* me of the story of Mary and Martha. There is so much in this short biblical narrative. I think we barely scratch the surface when we relegate these two amazing women to simply having different personalities.

While obviously it is true that they may have been different in nature, no one can be summed up in just one story from their life. Martha is more than the woman who chose to do the dishes when Jesus was in her home teaching and sharing mysteries. That being said, her story is so helpful to me on almost a daily basis.

The truth is, I am *both* Mary *and* Martha in that story. I think we all are. I have been on both sides of that story in different seasons of my life. I may not have had Jesus physically dining in my house with an entourage of His friends, but I have had lots of moments where I sensed His drawing, His presence calling me to come sit with Him, to look at Him, and I didn't.

Maybe you've had those moments, too. They present as seemingly small invitations to wake up earlier, go for a walk, take in the beauty of the sky, laugh with a baby, to resist heaviness and put on praise, or to release worry and take up faith-filled prayers. I have often wondered why God gave us freewill when it leads to us choosing lesser things, but the truth is that perfect love demands voluntary participation. If you can't say no, it's not voluntary, and if it's not voluntary, it's not really love.

Writing those words doesn't come without tears. To my core, I hate every *no* I have ever given God. Even though I'm thankful God has given me the option to say *no* (because without it my *yes* means nothing) I have never said *no* to Him and been glad I did. While I hate the *no,* I am so thankful that He remains faithful and uses it all for our good!

After Jesus led me out of the season of compromise I shared about in the previous chapter, the most pernicious fox I had to deal with was shame. Once I realized Jesus hated shame, I decided to do whatever it took to get free and stay free of it!

SHAME IN THE BEGINNING

When Adam and Eve were existing in the paradise of Eden, without spot or any awareness of darkness, God's nearness enveloped them. Therefore goodness enveloped them. They existed in an atmosphere of goodness—goodness from within, goodness around them—nothing but goodness. I often wonder about the heart-breaking moment when they felt something other than *goodness* for the very first time. We have lived in a fallen world our whole lives with no memory of a world without the presence of darkness. I can only imagine how horrific it must have felt, both spiritually and physically, for them.

Before they ate from the knowledge of good and evil, they had no knowledge of evil. They didn't understand or have any experience of what would happen when they ate the fruit. They had no frame of reference for darkness. Running and hiding wasn't an informed decision either. They had *never* hidden from God before, meaning it wasn't a learned behavior. For some reason it was now their instinct to hide and cover themselves. Why? I believe it's because shame was beginning to take root.

They weren't deceived into thinking that darkness was somehow more enticing or appealing—as is often the case for us, as well—because again, they had no reference for darkness. They did however have a deep awareness and experiential knowledge of goodness—of God Himself walking in unhindered relationship and partnership with them.

Believing that God was *not* good was the deception and darkness that took root in their hearts. They believed He was somehow withholding something that was beneficial (the knowledge of good and evil) even while they lived in the midst of the bliss of Eden. Even now, isn't this crafty lie concerning God's goodness still the crux of so many of the battles we face?

When they decided to not trust His goodness, they took their lives in their own hands. They pulled themselves out of a posture of surrender and partnership with God into a spirit of self-reliance and consequently self-protection. What does this look like in modern terms? I would suggest that self-protection is at play if you are living under the assumption that you need to toughen up, suck it up, pull up those boots straps and white knuckle it through life.

If you struggle to ask for help, to appear vulnerable, to not have an answer to a question, or to wait on God to move forward, then this ancient fox is likely running around your vineyard somewhere. Shame is a bully that will try and crush you into the ground, but self-protection falsely tries to inspire you into a place of confidence *without* God. Both are rooted in distrust of God.

This particular fox has been trying to make a home in my vineyard for as long as I can remember. One of my earliest memories, most likely around the age of six, I was alone in my room crying about some-thing. I wasn't just crying, I was suffering. I was experiencing that internal twisting that occurs with true heart break. As I sobbed, I remember thinking how much I hated that feeling, and then a sudden thought popped into my head. *Your feelings are like a faucet, and you could just turn it off.* I stopped crying at that moment and don't remember crying again until my first encounter with Jesus on the beach at thirteen. I chose in that moment to allow a false protection into my heart and life that has taken decades to dismantle.

You might be asking, "What's so wrong with protecting myself?" I'm not denying the reality that there is real pain and suffering in this life that we all experience in differing degrees and expressions. In those times, protecting yourself may be necessary and reasonable. However, if we allow self-protection to be a numbing agent to get us through hard times, that numbness will carry over into the good times. When we numb ourselves from pain, we numb ourselves to every other emotion as well. Again, foxes don't play fair. Something as seemingly innocuous as self-protection can easily metastasize into a huge road-block to intimacy with the Lord and those we love.

From the womb, we are intricately wired for connection, belonging, and vulnerability to one another. Many studies have been done showing the brain activity of infants in response to eye contact from loved ones and even strangers. It stimulates their brain in a unique way that lays the foundation for a healthy neural network physio-logically.[4]

Spiritually, we can see it in how God communicates to us who He is through the Bible and by His Spirit. He is not alone, and we are not meant to be alone. But aloneness and the perpetuation of aloneness that is self-reliance is a direct result of that initial deception concerning God's goodness. It is the fruit of shame which drives us into hiding—hiding from God, like Adam and Eve, and hiding from each other.

On that day when darkness first laid hands on the goodness of God's creation, when humanity felt its first pang of death's influence, we became less than intended. The shame of that moment became a veil that covered the goodness.

In the natural, Adam and Eve decided to fashion clothes—a new desire to cover up and create barriers between themselves and God and between each other. They suddenly felt a need to be hidden in some way. Skin was no longer enough. They felt exposed and uncomfortable and vulnerable, and so they covered themselves. There's no way to prove they had never felt these things, but it was certainly the first time they were trying to navigate them without God. And the most natural and simple solution they could come up with was fashioning clothes out of fig leaves.

This simple act speaks volumes about human nature. We are wired for connection, belonging, and vulnerability. *However,* we often resist those needs in our lives. Even the most emotionally intelligent and self-aware people are often in a battle with vulnerability and at most tolerate it's existence with a select few vetted and trusted others.

It makes sense to us that Adam and Eve covered themselves because we read the story from a physically clothed and figuratively covered existence. But for them, it was foreign. Covering was new. Covering was an adjustment. Covering was hiding. They were hiding under temporary, botanical clothing because spiritually they were experiencing shame for the first time—depth-exposing, soul-wrenching, sticky-tar-blanket shame.

Shame isn't the sadness we feel when we do something wrong. That's guilt, and guilt isn't in itself a bad thing. It is part of our God-given, internal compass that lets us know when we have violated the unspoken boundaries of those connections, tenuous social structures, and relationships we are hard-wired to exist within. Guilt is like a smoke alarm warning us that something is off and action is needed to preserve the structure of our relationships. Shame is different. Shame is insidious and deeply personal.

If guilt is a smoke alarm warning of potential danger within a structure, shame is a crack in the foundation allowing water to flood the basement, rotting the structure from within. It's harder to detect and can often be dressed up with caulk and new paint, but when shame is present, the whole structure is in danger of faltering from within. Shame is the lie that there is something fundamentally wrong with you, and self-protection is the desperate attempt to keep others away from your musty basement and cracked foundation.

If Adam and Eve had felt guilt rather than shame, they would have run to God rather than from Him. Certainly, once He came to them, guilt would have exposed the tenderness of their hearts and the desire to make it right, but it was shame that was at work. We can tell by the fruit it bore: blame, hiddenness, desperation, isolation, and excuses. When these things are present, we can be sure shame is at work.

Overcoming shame is a battle that every human fights—not because of anything we have done, but because of lies we have believed about who we are (or aren't). Shame is a slow death from the inside out. It chokes the very life out of us. *And isn't that exactly what God said would happen?*[5]

> *"When you eat from it, you shall surely die."*
>
> — Genesis 2:17, NKJV

When they ate it, they didn't suddenly, physically die—at least not in the sense that we experience bodily death. So what death was God speaking of? I believe it was a spiritual death, and shame was the cupbearer.

The gloriously good news here is that while this may be the beginning of the story, it isn't the end. We may have been born into a fallen world, but through Jesus and His Spirit living in us, there is now no condemnation![6] We have been and are being made new. If we let Him do His part, and we surrender to our part, His perfect love will mature us into a Bride free from shame!

Don't let shame write your story, Beloved. Resolve in your heart to say *yes* to the journey of ridding your life of shame.

Jesus, I ask You to help us lock eyes with You today! Help us to feel the heat of Your gaze and receive the fullness of Your love for us. Burn away every hidden foxhole within that makes room for shame. I ask You to give us grace to surrender to the process, say yes to your leadership, and kick shame out of our vineyards! Expand our hearts to receive Your thoughts about us, and give us courage to believe them!

CHAPTER SUMMARY

- Jesus hates shame.
- An aversion to eye contact can be evidence of shame. Jesus wants to hold our gaze and melt away the shame.
- Shame is different from guilt. Guilt says you did something wrong. Shame says *you* are wrong.
- Shame seeks to isolate us by tempting us to hide from God and others.
- When Adam and Eve experienced death and disconnection from God, shame was present. They hid from God and each other for the first time.
- The inheritance of shame from the fall of man in Eden isn't the end of the story. Jesus took all our shame on the cross when He was fully laid bare, arms wide open.

QUESTIONS FOR REFLECTION

1. What does "eye contact" with the Creator feel like for you? Try and describe it in word or picture form.

2. Sit with Holy Spirit for a moment in silence. Just *be* with Him, and acknowledge that He is God. He is your Creator.

Now acknowledge that He is also fiercely, stubbornly, and relentlessly in love with you. Ask Him to tell you how He feels and write down what you hear. Acknowledge any resistance you have to those words.

3. Ask the Holy Spirit if the fox called shame has made a home in your vineyard. Are there tunnels dug out beneath the surface that undermine the foundation of who you are? If those tunnels had statements written on them about you, what would they say?

4. Shame thrives in the dark. Exposing it to the light of truth kills it. Ask Holy Spirit what the truth has always been about you since He created you? Write it. Speak it. I encourage you to find a creative way to tell the story of who you are from your Creator's perspective. Write a poem. Paint a picture. Make a collage. Whatever comes to mind, don't hesitate. Just do it! And then find someone to share it with.

----

1. See Matthew 6:22, TPT.
2. "Eye Contact Detection in Humans from Birth - Researchgate." Accessed November 8, 2021. https://www.researchgate.net/publication/11293433_Eye_-contact_detection_in_humans_from_birth.
3. says:, Rachel, EMoon says: Anonymous says: Andrew Maxey says: Jess Kelly says: Adult Psychology Says: Shoes Shed says: et al. "Why Do Children Hide by Covering Their Eyes?" Research Digest, November 3, 2016. https://digest.bp-s.org.uk/2012/10/23/why-do-children-hide-by-covering-their-eyes/.
4. "Social Relationships and Health - Science.sciencemag.org." Accessed November 8, 2021. https://science.sciencemag.org/content/241/4865/540/tab-article-info.
5. "Then the Lord God took the man and put him in the garden of Eden to tend and keep it. And the Lord God commanded the man, saying, "Of every tree of the garden you may freely eat; but of the tree of the knowledge of good and evil you shall not eat, for in the day that you eat of it you shall surely die." Genesis 2:15-17, NKJV
6. *"So now the case is closed.* There remains no accusing voice of condemnation against those who are joined in life-union with Jesus, the Anointed One." Romans 8:1, TPT

CHAPTER 10

THE FOX CALLED FEAR

" But we are certainly not those who are held back by fear and perish; we are among those who have faith and experience true life!"

— HEBREWS 10:39, TPT

I am a dreamer. My whole life I have had multiple dreams a night, and God often uses them to start conversations with me or offer guidance. I do my best to journal most of them because I have so many that they are easy to forget. There have however been a handful of dreams where God spoke so powerfully that I fell out of bed and shook under His presence. Those dreams leave impressions that mark and mold my heart.

This is one of those dreams:

I was driving in my hunter green Jeep Cherokee, which was my first car. In real life, I loved that car and drove it until it died. In the dream, I was driving along with a map in my hand that I had drawn of the Scottish Highlands. (It just so happens, that week I had drawn this exact map as part of an assignment for a college course.) As I

*drove I was confused because the map didn't match where I was. I
knew I wasn't in the Scottish Highlands, so the map couldn't help me.*

*Suddenly, the presence of God entered the car! It's hard to explain
what it was like, but the best I can offer was it felt like the fear of the
Lord.¹ I was struck with such instant awe that I fell to the floor of the
car. I was tucked in a ball, covering my head, under the steering
column. If I could have pulled up the carpet lining to get under it, I
would have.*

*I did this duck and cover in response to His presence as I was driving,
and this thought went through my head, "Oh no! Who's driving the
car?"*

*Then God spoke audibly in response to my thought and said, "Don't
you think I can drive a car?"*

His voice shook me to my core, and I literally fell out of my bed and
woke up when I hit the ground. I laid with my face to the ground, in
the middle of my bedroom, in the middle of the night, shaking under
His presence.

I don't know how long I laid there trembling, but in the morning God
began to unpack the short but powerful dream to me. He has referenced it over the years to address the issue of fear in my life.

EXPOSING THE SPIRIT OF FEAR

One of the things that stands out to me from that dream is that I was
initially using a map I had drawn myself that wasn't of the country I
was driving in. How often do we live our lives on autopilot,
consulting the self-constructed maps of where we think we are or
where we should be going, only to realize we are completely lost? I've
heard fear described before as *False Evidence Appearing Real.* One of the
hallmarks of the spirit of fear is a distorting of reality. Allowing fear a

place of influence in your life is like consulting a map for a country you're not even in.

The other thing that stands out is that the fear of the Lord causes us to bow in reverence. It puts things into perspective. He gets magnified, and we understand we are His creation—not the other way around. The spirit of fear will try and distort your perception of reality to get you off course, but the fear of the Lord will reorient you with the one TRUE reality and put you back on course. It's the beginning of wisdom.[2]

When God spoke, "Don't you think I can drive a car?" He wasn't just giving me information. There were layers of revelation in His words, as there always is. I knew that He was asking me if I trusted Him. Did I trust Him to get me where I needed to go and to get me there safely?

Safety is not a bad thing unless it becomes an idol and allows the spirit of fear access to your heart. We are conditioned from an early age to exalt safety and protect our lives and bodies from harm. In the dream, that conditioning for safety looked like me worrying even while I was plastered to the floor of the car, overwhelmed with God's presence. (Worrying about your safety isn't wisdom when God's presence is surrounding you!) How often do we declare that He is our provider and our protector, and then let fear tell us we are going to crash and burn?

I have found over the years that the fox named fear is the sidekick to shame. Shame is the bully that tries to constantly put you in your place. Fear is his chatty minion that tries to keep you there. Shame will make you doubt yourself, while fear will make you doubt everything and everyone around you.

On some level we allow fear to hang around when we think it's working on our behalf. Maybe it's keeping you from making too many mistakes, embarrassing yourself, or taking unnecessary risks, but it's not your friend. It's not your protector. It's a fox, looking for a free meal. And it will turn on you if given the chance.

THE ENEMY OF MY ENEMY IS MY FRIEND

We know from scripture that the enemy of fear is love:

> *"Love never brings fear, for fear is always related to punishment. But love's perfection drives the fear of punishment far from our hearts. Whoever walks constantly afraid of punishment has not reached love's perfection."*

> — 1 JOHN 4:18

When we are walking out the Shulamite's journey of maturing love, we are at war with fear. Perfect love won't bring punishment. It might bring unknowns and opportunities that lead to failure or disappointment, but never punishment. Perfect Love may ask you to run into the unknown upon the mountains, and you may skin your knee along the way, but you can be sure it will all be used for your good. Fear was never meant to be your companion. Perfect Love Himself is your partner in this journey.

Running with Jesus and allowing the flow of the Creator to move through your life will open up your life, not diminish it. Fear would tell us that if we really give everything to God it will limit our options and that we will be put in a religious cage and stripped of our freedom. But the truth is we only find freedom in Him. When we give our full *yes* and let go of the parts of our life we are so desperately trying to hold onto, Jesus opens up our lives to a world of possibilities. I have seen this at play in my creative process of painting.

When fear is present with an artist, you can see it by the limitations in supplies, tools, techniques, or expressions they are willing to ignore. They put themselves in a sort of "creativity prison" with rules and regulations that must be followed. The problem with letting fear speak is that the creative process is significantly hindered. Assuming we push fear aside long enough to get out of the gate, we will find hurdle after hurdle holding us back from the authentic expression we long for.

In my students' lives, fear looks like them putting a tiny squirt of paint on their pallet because they are scared to use too much. Or perhaps they limit themselves to only a few colors. Or maybe they sit quietly when they paint and reach for a small paintbrush that they can hold like a pencil and have more control over. All of these actions are indicators of fear-based thinking.

The most freedom I have found in painting is when I am worshiping wildly, singing, dancing, and swaying. I choose canvases that are big with lots of room to play, brushes that are big and lots of different shapes, and paint that is fluid and difficult to control. I intentionally throw paint on the canvas without thinking too much about where I'm going. It's a way of me trusting the process.

I decided a long time ago that I trust God and my heart to move through the creative process and deal with whatever comes along. I trust that what the painting is supposed to become will reveal itself as I paint. That kind of freedom can be lived out in our everyday lives when we choose to let go of fear and embrace the process. Dismantle the illusion of control, and just learn to play again!

This kind of care-free living may seem impossible in reality. There might be a part of you that thinks this kind of idealism is in the clouds, unattainable. But I would challenge you to think about your Bridegroom. Think about the One who leaps upon the mountains like a gazelle.[3] Think about the One whose burden is light—who laughs when the nations rage![4]

Fear has zero hold on Jesus' heart. In His light there is only light—no shadow of turning.[5] He is our perfect example and the One with whom we will be in covenant forever. If He is free from fear, then it is a reality in God and possible for our hearts, as well!

CHAPTER SUMMARY

- The fear of the Lord is the beginning of wisdom. The spirit of fear tries to alter reality, but the spirit of the fear of the Lord resets us to the one true reality.

- Fear and shame work together. Shame is the bully that tries to put you in your place. Fear is it's minion that tries to keep you there.
- Fear is the enemy of perfect love.
- Fear in the midst of creative process will hold you back from authentic expression.
- Jesus isn't afraid of anything. Ever. Being free from fear is a reality in God.

QUESTIONS FOR REFLECTION

1. Sit with the Holy Spirit, and make a list of all the fears you currently carry. Ask Him what you should do with that list. Follow His lead whatever it may be. Consider destroying it or turning it into a piece of art.

2. What is your experience with the fear of the Lord? It isn't a topic that is discussed often in the Western Church. Read through Matthew 10 and meditate on verses 26-28. Ask the Holy Spirit to give you insight. Write down what He tells you.

EXTRA CREDIT

One of the workshops I teach is called "Abstract Florals." In this three hour workshop, I walk students through doing a quick wash-background with watercolor or thinned out acrylic that takes no more than ten minutes to apply and blend. While that dries, we soak in God's presence for ten to twenty minutes while listening to worship music and asking the Holy Spirit to talk to us about what kind of flower our heart is like.

Then I lead them in a finger-painting exercise that God had me do on stage one night when I was painting during worship. I have them pick four colors for their flower and put a different color on each finger, starting with the darkest color on the pointer finger and moving towards the lighter color on the pinky. I have them put yellow on their thumb. Then I have them make messy circular shapes working one finger at a time, from the darkest color to the lightest. The yellow on the thumb is then dotted in the center of the flower and acts as an anchor of sorts, informing the brain that this abstract shape is floral.

I challenge you to do this exercise, or some form of finger painting, while talking to Holy Spirit. It doesn't matter if you've ever held a paintbrush. You don't even need to own a paintbrush; you've got ten attached to your hands! Finger painting may seem childish, but it is a powerful tool for opening our hearts to the joy of playing with our Creator. There is no goal in this exercise other than having fun and being kind to yourself. If at any point you feel yourself being unkind, pause and ask Holy Spirit His thoughts. Then agree with Him.

---

1. "The starting point for acquiring wisdom is to be consumed with awe as you worship Jehovah-God. To receive the revelation of the Holy One, you must come to the one who has living-understanding." Proverbs 9:10, TPT
2. See Psalm 111:10.
3. "Let me describe him: he is graceful as a gazelle, swift as a wild stag. Now he comes closer, even to the places where I hide. He gazes into my soul, peering through the portal as he blossoms within my heart." SOS 2:9, TPT
4. See Matthew 11:30, Psalm 2.
5. "Every gift God freely gives us is good and perfect, streaming down from the Father of lights, who shines from the heavens with no hidden shadow or darkness and is never subject to change." James 1:17, TPT

CHAPTER 11

THE FOX CALLED COMPARISION

"Look at the splendor of your skies, your creative genius glowing in the heavens. When I gaze at your moon and your stars, mounted like jewels in their settings, I know you are the fascinating artist who fashioned it all! But when I look up and see such wonder and workmanship above, I have to ask you this question: Compared to all this cosmic glory, why would you bother with puny, mortal man or be infatuated with Adam's sons? Yet what honor you have given to men, created only a little lower than Elohim, crowned like kings and queens with glory and magnificence. You have delegated to them mastery over all you have made, making everything subservient to their authority, placing earth itself under the feet of your image-bearers."

— Psalm 8:3-6

Comparison. Let's just all take a deep breath before we jump into this. This fox is sly. It is cunning. It is a survivalist.

Comparison is the ability to hold one thing next to another and acknowledge how they are alike and different. It is a skill with lots of practical and useful applications in life. But one area it is entirely *unhelpful* is art. In my opinion art in any medium can't be compared. Not one work to another, and certainly not one artist to another because the standard for what an artist could be is within them.

To that point, we are God's workmanship and all individual works of art. Comparing one of God's masterpieces to another makes as much sense as trying to compare a Van Gogh to a Jackson Pollock. DaVinci's *Mona Lisa* is beautiful in and of itself. It doesn't become more or less so when compared to Monet's *Waterlilies*. As God's artwork, the only standard we have to compare ourselves to is Jesus and the potential within us.

When I was about nine years old in the fourth grade, my class went on a field trip to the roller-skating rink. It was always my favorite field trip, and I looked forward to it every year. The fun music, the disco lights, the hot spinning churros and slushies from the snack counter— I loved everything about it.

Towards the end of the day they announced they were going to start the races categorized by age. The winner would receive a token to the snack bar. I could taste the churro already. There was no question in mind—I had this. Without hesitation I hurried to the floor and got in line as my age group was called. I looked down the line and sized up my competition. I put my skate to the line and waited for the pop gun to go off and the music to start signaling the start of the race. The DJ on the booming loudspeaker reminded us to wait for the start, no pushing would be tolerated, if you hit a cone marking the course you're out, and if you fall down move to the side so as not to be run over.

You could hear a pin drop as the line of ready skaters posed in anticipation. "Ready! Set!" A teenage rink attendant called out with the cap gun above his head. "POP!"

The music started blaring as nine-year-old feet furiously scuffled off the starting line. The race was two laps around the oval rink. I quickly put distance between me and the others. I made sure to squat low and lean as I rounded the corners as close to those orange traffic cones as I could get without hitting one. The wind in my face, the loud music and cheering—it was all so exhilarating.

As I finished my first lap and started the second, I saw other racers off to the side of the course or quickly crawling out of the lane. Some were crying, and some were struggling to stand as they pulled themselves up on the carpeted walls of the rink. I continued to skate as fast as I could, nearing the last corner before the finish. I started to wonder if I was the only one left in the race. I looked over my left shoulder to see if anyone was behind me. No one was there! I couldn't believe it. My churro victory was almost in hand! I extended out of my squatting race posture and began to coast the last stretch of the course.

Suddenly a flash of stone-washed denim and pigtails flew by my right side! She had been in my blind spot and my choice to slow down gave her the advantage she needed. I fumbled to respond as she skated full-speed ahead across the finish line and the crowd cheered for the sudden upset.

That loss stuck with me. The thing is, if I had tried my best and pigtails had still beat me, that would have been one thing...but I didn't do my best. I slowed down at the end because I decided I didn't have to try my best if there wasn't any competition. More than anything I was just embarrassed I didn't give it my all. I compared myself to the other racers and my effort was based on them. God doesn't call us to run our race of life in this manner. He calls us to run the race that is marked out before *us* without worrying about how others are doing or where their path is taking them.

> "As for us, we have all of these great witnesses who encircle us like clouds. So we must **let go of every wound** that has pierced us and the sin we so easily fall into. Then we will be able to run life's marathon race with passion and determination, for **the path has been already marked out before us.**"

> — Hebrews 12:1, TPT (emphasis added)

In life, we aren't competing against those around us. The only real competition we face is within us. It's the wounds and sins that ensnare us. It's comparison that trips us up and gets us to try and run someone else's race. But God has laid out the path for us. If we say *yes* to letting go of our wounds and following His lead on the path He lays out, then we've already won.

COMPARISON IS A SHAPESHIFTER

Comparison can be a hard fox to catch because sometimes it disguises itself as other things: logic, reason, wisdom, discernment, compassion, and so on. It's veiled judgment—judgment of others, judgment of ourselves, and ultimately it becomes judgment of God. It's ugly, and it's not a part of God's Kingdom.

Comparison can sound like truth, and it might even be a twisted up misapplied version of the truth. It can sound like:

- Comparing yourself to the "future you"— "I'm not ready for that opportunity...maybe in five to ten years."
- Comparing yourself with someone else— "Someone else could do this better. I should step aside."
- Comparing seasons— "They are getting all the opportunities I wish I had."
- Comparing others with your experience—"Why can't that guy find a job? I wonder how hard he's *actually* trying. I've never had a hard time finding a job."
- Comparing yourself with the fantasy that others just have it easier—"I just don't have what it takes to do that. I wasn't born with that talent."

Did a few of those sound familiar and make you cringe? Comparison sounds harmless when it's in our heads. It seems like a helpful tool for coping, or assessing, or distancing ourselves from pain. However, when we bring those thoughts out into the light, we see them for what they are—*an ugly attempt to be our own god.*

Comparison is a shoddy at best, destructive at worst, attempt to create a safe place to shelter us from pain, disappointment, and disillusionment. I pray that you have safe people in your life that you can go to when you need to process negative emotions, but even if you don't, ultimately God is the safest place to run.

> *"The character of God is a tower of strength, for the lovers of God delight to run into his heart and be exalted on high."*
>
> — Proverbs 18:10

When we are allowing comparison to tell us how to assess a situation, we are inviting the hierarchies of this world to govern our lives. We are deciding who matters and who doesn't, who is good and who is bad. God's Kingdom is built upon His character and ways. He doesn't compare us one to another.

There are no hierarchies in His Kingdom. It's just God the Creator and His creation. Even the way He has extended an invitation across that gap is astounding! He completely leveled the playing field when He died for us. We are all under *His* blood because *none of us* could do it on our own, and yet, at the same time, we are all standing in *His* righteousness! We've all fallen short, but the same invitation for relationship with Him is extended to all of us!

If it's so obviously wrong, so glaringly ugly when we really look at it, why do we do it so often and so easily? We do it because it's learned. It's familiar. It feels like a quick fix to a nuanced problem or a shot of comfort when we want to avoid the process of running our own race with endurance. It's a distraction at best, a complete detour from your race at worst.

Comparing our lives, bodies, success, even spiritual walks is the message we receive over and over and a system of behavior we learn to accept from this world. It's a symptom of the kingdom of this world that promotes independence, success, and happiness above all else. In some cultures and organizations it's the air they breathe. Learning to live free from comparison can feel like breathing a new substance at first. Jarring. Disorienting. Like a life-long smoker quitting and regaining their sense of smell—we don't realize what comparison has cost us until we start to live free from it.

COMPARATIVE SUFFERING

I remember a conversation I had with a roommate in college one evening in which she wondered aloud if others just experience life as "easier" than others. She was a deep thinker who was passionate about social justice, and she lived a beautifully authentic life from what I observed. I enjoyed her friendship and respected her thoughts and opinions.

As we talked, she described to me some of the things she had seen in third world countries on mission trips and some stories of personal tragedy and trauma she had experienced in her own life. She expressed her struggle to understand those who just seem to lead a happy, care-free life. Her struggle was real and messy, and she was present to it. This is the kind of conversation I love to engage in with friends and the Holy Spirit. Honest. Raw. Authentic. Messy.

We went back and forth for a while, sharing our shared confusion on the matter, our guilt over living such blessed lives compared to some, and yet our deep wounds from childhood that others just didn't seem to carry. Eventually, we settled on there just being a dynamic tension, a mystery to life, in which each person's individual experience is all they know. Pain is pain, we concluded. We didn't have an answer, but talking about it helped. It helped me begin to put words to the pain I felt around this topic of comparative suffering.

Using someone else's suffering to diminish my own was effective in helping me feel better, but something felt profoundly wrong about it.

That's because the opposite of comparison is empathy and compassion, and empathy and compassion are profoundly right. Using someone else's pain as a measuring stick to our own isn't helpful or healthy. Rather, it is the heart of God that we lean in and bear burdens with one another, seeking to understand one another and help those who are hurting or in need.

Comparing our suffering breeds distance, not closeness—not burden-bearing love. When we use someone else's pain as a temporary sedative to our own, we are numbing not just our pain, but our empathy as well. Empathy happens when we seek to understand another and are willing to enter into the emotional state they are experiencing.[1] Compassion is similar, but it also seeks to help.

Jesus was often moved with compassion when it came to the suffering of others.[2] How profoundly backwards it is for us as followers of Jesus to use someone else's suffering in some twisted way to help ourselves, rather than helping them. But that's exactly what the fox of comparison leads us into.

THE SEEDS OF COMPARISON

When I read the Gospels and learn about the wild life Jesus and his ragtag team of followers lived, I am often struck by two things. First, I envy the front row seat the disciples had to Jesus and my heart aches at the thought of seeing Him in action as closely as they did. Second, I don't envy how the disciples' lives, including their mistakes, have been used for centuries by the church to help us understand our own walks with the Lord.

They were just people. They were doing their best to understand who this mysterious Man was, this Man they dropped everything to follow. This man of miracles, who touched lepers, wasn't afraid to associate with prostitutes and tax collectors. This humble, kind, unassuming man, who spoke with such truth and grace, easily captivated spiritually hungry crowds with His depth of wisdom and amazing love.

He turned water into wine, raised people from the dead, fearlessly stood up to the religious elite, and even overturned tables like a madman in the temple. He was safe and disarming, but also "other-than," like no other. How could they possibly understand that He was Yahweh? The very one who *created* them was walking with them through the hills of Israel, making camp with them, breaking bread with them.

What a profound honor to have lived in that time and walked with Jesus, to see the expression on His face when He healed someone, and to hear the inflection in His tone. And yet, we can see the seeds of comparison causing conflict and division among the disciples along the way.

Multiple times the Gospels record the disciples arguing over who would be the greatest in the Kingdom. I can't help but wonder if this comparison was able to make its home in the disciples' hearts because they didn't yet have a full understanding of the man they were following. But then again, believers now have the same issues.

This nagging plague of comparison messed with the disciples all the way to the very end when Jesus ascended up into the heavens. After Jesus was resurrected, there is an intimate scene laid out in the Gospel of John where Jesus meets them at the Sea of Galilee.[3] The disciples were out fishing, and they saw Him on the shore but didn't recognize Him.

Jesus called out to them and asked if they'd caught anything; they hadn't. Then He told them to cast their nets again, and they began to pull in a huge catch of fish that took all the disciples to pull it in. When Peter realized it was Jesus, he dropped his nets and ran for Him.

This was right after Peter had denied Jesus three times, and he was suffering with the shame of his denial. Jesus performs this miracle catch of fish which would have reminded Peter of his initial invitation to follow Jesus that we read about in Luke 5:2-10. I relate to Peter in this story, having had my own denial moment that left its mark, followed by an invitation to "pick up where we left off" from Jesus. He so kindly and generously offered Peter redemption in that moment. He restored him fully and then recommissioned him to feed His sheep.

Immediately following this redemptive moment, Jesus told Peter that he was destined to die as a martyr. Peter replied by asking about John's future. Jesus's reply cuts straight to the point: *"If I decide to let him live until I return, what concern is that of yours? You must still keep on following me!"*[4] As soon as Peter was restored, the maturing process began. That process distinctly allowed no room for comparison.

No matter what exploits you may accomplish in your lifetime, the greatest assignment you will have is the one given to Peter—love Jesus, and feed His sheep. You have a specific path laid out for your race. You are called to accomplish your heavenly assignment in your own unique way. You can't afford to worry what "the guy in the other lane" is doing. You must settle the matter in the secret place and decide that you will stay in your lane, surrender to God's leadership, and do *your* best, regardless of the audience.

Your competition is against your flesh and everything that hinders your love. There is no one to compare yourself to other than Jesus. He is the Way—the perfect example to us of what it is to be fully human! So put your blinders on if you have to until your heart is free. Let Jesus be your only plumb line, and give comparison no room to dwell in your vineyard!

CHAPTER SUMMARY

- Comparison leads to compromise and not running your race to the best of your ability.

- Comparison can disguise itself as logic, reason, wisdom, discernment, compassion, and even sympathy.
- We are all unique masterpieces made by the Master Artist. There is no comparison in His Kingdom. If you are comparing yourself to another person, you are not partnering with God's Kingdom.
- Comparison is a form of judgment against God.
- Jesus leveled the playing field when He died for us. He is the standard. Everyone is saved by grace, through faith.
- When we allow comparative suffering to diminish our pain, we diminish our empathy as well.

QUESTIONS FOR REFLECTION

1. How has the comparison fox affected you? Ask the Holy Spirit to show you any ways in which comparison has been recently masquerading as a welcome guest in your vineyard?

2. Read through Mark 9, and put yourself in the shoes of the disciples. Would you rather have been one of the disciples that was chosen to go up to the Mount of Transfiguration or the ones left behind who endured a failed deliverance session and then public rebuke? Ask Holy Spirit to unpack this chapter to you and help you apply it to any area of your life necessary.

3. One of the best ways to trap the fox of comparison is to act in the opposite spirit. If there is someone in your life that you find yourself comparing yourself to, ask the Lord for a way to secretly bless them. Instead of focusing on where you feel you might be lacking, look for ways to promote others and celebrate their victories and accomplishments! Ask God for opportunities this week to trade comparison for generous love, and then lavish it on others freely!

1. "Celebrate with those who celebrate, and weep with those who grieve." Romans 12:15, TPT
2. See Matthew 9:36, Matthew 14:14, Matthew 20:34, Mark 1:41, Luke 10:33, John 11:33.
3. See John 21.
4. See John 21:22, TPT.

CHAPTER 12

THE FOX CALLED REJECTION

"And he chose us to be his very own, joining us to himself even before he laid the foundation of the universe! Because of his great love, he ordained us, so that we would be seen as holy in his eyes with an unstained innocence. For it was always in his perfect plan to adopt us as his delightful children, through our union with Jesus, the Anointed One, so that his tremendous love that cascades over us would glorify his grace—for the same love he has for his Beloved One, Jesus, he has for us. And this unfolding plan brings him great pleasure!"

— EPHESIANS 1:4-6

Have you ever noticed that the stories that are most personal, the ones we try and guard the heaviest, are often the most universal? In today's modern times we can live completely disconnected from one another and believe that our stories of rejection, pain, and shame are somehow exclusive to us. This simply isn't so. We have all experienced pain, loss, and rejection in our lives—some more than others—but no one escapes this life, no matter how privileged their existence may seem, without a few sob stories. It's the very stories we often try to forget or hide from one another that can actually empower us to grow into our destiny.

> *"My fellow believers, when it seems as though you are facing nothing but difficulties, see it as an invaluable opportunity to experience the greatest joy that you can! For you know that when your faith is tested it stirs up power within you to endure all things. And then as your endurance grows even stronger it will release perfection into every part of your being until there is nothing missing and nothing lacking."*
>
> — JAMES 1:2-4, TPT

In the midst of a trial, especially one involving rejection, it can feel minimizing to hear that it's an opportunity to learn something. And if you are in the middle of a trial right now, I would say take the time you need to feel your way through it, but when you are able, allow the Lord to gently guide you through the process of gleaning gold from the wreckage. He wastes nothing. He redeems all things. Even the most devastating of blows can be used for your good if you lean on Him through it. Ultimately, as His bride, we are being made ready, and because of that process, we can expect that every bitter thing will be made sweet.[1]

Have you ever wondered why God made our bodies to function the way we do? The fact that we are able to sense pain, both physical *and* emotional, is a profound mystery. The nervous system, comprising your brain, spinal cord, and a network of neurons, can transmit information at speeds of almost four hundred feet per second. If you were to stretch out the neural network that exists within you, it would be over ninety thousand miles of sensations![2] The earth is only 24,901 miles in circumference, so this means your neural network could circle the earth over three and a half times!

Surely, the God who made such a complex system for delivering and storing information about our experiences in this life can help us process the profound and universal sting of rejection.

THE FIRST CUT IS THE DEEPEST

For the longest time, my first memory was of the morning I found out my parents were getting a divorce. My six-year-old legs climbed up onto my dad's lap where I sat innocently as he watched TV in a daze. I had a stomach ache because I was nervous to ask him what was burning in my heart. I finally found the courage and asked if he and my mom were getting a divorce. I remember the suffocating feeling of power those words had. They shifted the room and couldn't be unsaid.

His pause and facial expression told me that what was coming wasn't good. The churning in my stomach increased. He turned off the TV and called my mom in the room. At that point, my surroundings tunnelled. It was as if the room I was in no longer existed, and all I can remember was the information being given to me and my thoughts about it.

The memory written in that moment shifted from looking outside myself to the smaller, safer space within me. I was going inward and searching for escape. As they explained their plan to separate, they attempted to cushion the blow as best they could. They were crying, and obviously had planned to tell us, but because I was the one who brought it up, I felt responsible on some level.

The next morning my Dad moved out.

I can still feel the warm cement driveway under my bare feet as I watched him drive away. My mom, sister, and I stood in the driveway until his light blue car disappeared to the end of the street and around the corner. I don't think any of us knew what to do except cry.

I felt such an intense emotional pain that physically it registered as pain all over my body. My mind couldn't comprehend the life ahead because I had only known life with both of my parents under one roof. I loved my Dad so much, and though it wasn't his intention, his leaving felt like rejection. Deeply personal rejection.

That perceived experience of rejection became a defining moment for me. Being so young, it was part of the foundation that I built my understanding of the world upon. It has caused a lot of pain in my life. Pain that I wish I hadn't felt. I'm not glad that it happened, but in the long process of unpacking those experiences colored by rejection, I have found something invaluable—my *acceptance* as God's Beloved. Jesus has met me in my dark moments time and time again, and shown me how accepted I have always been and how fully known and wanted I am to Him.

Beloved, you don't need to experience rejection to learn your acceptance, but in case rejection, or even perceived rejection, has left its mark on you, I want to say to you that right now, in this moment, nothing is truer than your *acceptance* in Jesus. I know from my own experience that He can go with you to those rejection-soaked memories and tell you the truth about them. He can rewrite your story with you from Heaven's perspective.

What does rejection have to do with running with Jesus or His creative process? Everything. If we are to arise and run with Jesus in the fullness of our calling in this hour, we must conquer the crippling stories of rejection that we carry around with us and hide behind. In the Song of Songs chapter two the Shulamite says: *"Let me describe him: he is graceful as a gazelle, swift as a wild stag. Now he comes closer, even to the places where I hide. He gazes into my soul, peering through the portal as he blossoms within my heart. The one I love calls to me"* (Song of Songs 2:9-10, TPT).

When we choose Jesus, we are choosing to walk with the One who is *"graceful as a gazelle, swift as a wild stag."* Beneath this poetic imagery, there is a beautiful description of a man who is completely free. He is graceful, swift, and wild. There is no shadow in Him, holding Him back. The distortions of the enemy and the false narratives of life have no hold on Him. He is Truth incarnate, full of grace. He is the Way, swiftly dealing with the divine separation we could not conquer. He is the Life, wild and free, captive only to His chosen covenant of love. And He comes in close, even to the places where you hide.

OUT OF HIDING AND INTO ACCEPTANCE

Those places of hiding may look different for all of us, but many times the root is the same: rejection. The pain of past rejections leaves a mark, and your powerful brain does its job and tries to protect you from future harm. When you touch a stove that is hot, your brain creates a neural pathway that now connects the acts of touching heat with the sensation of pain. When you open your heart in vulnerability to another, and the result is painful for one reason or another, a similar unconscious correlation can be made.

Your amazing nervous system takes the information in the stored traumatic memory and tries to create a new barrier of protection. Unfortunately, that barrier doesn't just shield you from those that would harm you. Yes, it walls out potential harm, but it also walls you in. Jesus is on the other side of that wall, honoring the free will He gave you.

Right now, Beloved, He is coming in close, gazing into your soul, calling to you. He is saying, *"Arise, my dearest. Hurry, my darling. Come away with me!"* (Song of Songs 2:10 TPT). If your immediate reaction isn't "yes!" there is likely some level of self-protection causing you to tread lightly.

Perhaps one the most heartbreaking lines in scripture is the Shulamite's reply to the Bridegroom-King's first invitation: *"I'll come away another time"* (Song of Songs 2:17, TPT). The greatest pain I have experienced in my life didn't come from others rejecting me—it came from compromise that *I chose* to enter into. I rejected myself and abandoned my promises and values. These choices were the fruit of the perceived rejection I had experienced all those years back as a child.

When you let rejection define you, Jesus's offer of perfect love and bouncing around like a gazelle seems too good to be true, even silly. When we allow the rejection from others to stay in our vineyard, we are in essence giving that fox permission to make a home in us, and the result will be a cycle of future self-rejection.

Perhaps you've been there. Maybe you understand the Shulamite's reply. She liked what they had, but she wasn't yet willing to fully surrender to His call. That might look like a small compromise or an overt sin, but it might also look like excuses and qualifiers that talk you out of believing in the promises Jesus has spoken to your heart. It might look like you saying, *"No, this isn't the right time for me to start that business, buy those paints, write the book...I'll do it...later."*

I want to propose to you that maybe the thing that's holding you back from running isn't time, money, or skill. It could be those sly foxes of shame, fear, comparison, and rejection that we have discussed in these past few chapters nibbling at the fruit in your garden. Your fruit is meant to feed others.

Self-rejection is a sly fox that will limit you, causing you to play small, hold back, and never surrender fully to the wholehearted abandon of living like Jesus. Procrastination will find a way to push away every opportunity for growth. New experiences will be disallowed and life will become a cage. This is the opposite of what Jesus wants for you, the opposite of what He died to give you.

There are countless examples of Jesus loving those whom the world rejected. Mary Magdalene was filled with demons until Jesus embraced her.[3] Matthew the tax collector was despised, and Jesus asked him to be a disciple. Zacchaeus, the woman caught in adultery, the woman at the well—all were rejected by society, yet accepted by Jesus.[4]

If those aren't good enough company to be amongst, Jesus Himself was rejected beyond comprehension. He walked among His creation and they flat-out rejected Him. He truly is our high priest who can relate to every pain we have experienced.

He can even relate to the intense pressure of the systems of this world. This world worships hierarchies of every kind, including corporate ladders and power structures. Unfortunately this dynamic has even worked its way into many of our churches, pitting brother and sister against each other, causing us to jockey for positions and platforms, just like the lost.

Jesus knows what it's like to feel the pull of those intoxicating systems that thrive in comparison. He was constantly being pressured to be the person the world wanted Him to be, but He chose to hold the line and only do what He saw the Father doing. He stayed the course and ran the race the Father set before Him.

Likewise, using Jesus as our example, we must push aside every voice that would compare us to another. We must lock into what we hear the Father saying and doing. We will never find our way to the path that's been laid out for our race by looking at another path.

Having brothers and sisters to run alongside is a gift and can offer much encouragement and strength to help us run our race, but we have to be clear what our assignments are, where they overlap with those around us, and where the paths part ways. Jesus walked with the disciples, but He didn't let them, or anyone else, sway Him from the path the Father laid out for His life.

YOU'RE NOT ALONE

Beloved, the process of ridding your vineyard of the fruit stealing foxes is ongoing. Don't be overwhelmed by their presence. In fact, don't even try to figure it out when you become aware of their presence. If Holy Spirit is highlighting a fox, it is an invitation to remove that fox *with Him*. All you need to do when you want to be rid of a fox is look to Holy Spirit and ask for His help. It might be immediate, or it might be a process, but you will never be alone!

When the Bridegroom King alerts the Shulamite to the foxes that are hindering their love, he doesn't point a finger and demand she fix the problem. Rather, he says they will *do it together.*[5] An invitation like this shouldn't be ignored or taken lightly. If Holy Spirit is highlighting the foxes in your vineyard, it's an invitation to partnership, and that is a precious thing. I encourage you to say yes, even if you don't know what all it may entail.

Likewise, if He brings along godly people who see you the way He does and are offering to run with you and help you in this journey, *take it seriously!* If for some reason you don't have trusted spiritual leaders in your life that you can journey with, I highly recommend reaching out to Bethel Church's SOZO ministry.[6] They can help you gain clarity about the glorious partnership with Holy Spirit you are called to.

This book in your hand may very well be the evidence of His invitation to catch some foxes. I know from experience that those seasons may be intense, and the pruning might feel painful at times, but it is all unto freedom and wholeness. The abundant life that was won for you on the cross is final, and it is fully attained through the process of maintaining your vineyard.

CHAPTER SUMMARY

- God wastes nothing. He redeems all things. Even the most devastating blows can be used for your good.
- Nothing is truer than your acceptance in Jesus.
- When we allow the rejection of others to make a home in our vineyard, the result is cycles of self-rejection.
- Jesus made a point of seeking out those rejected by society.
- Jesus was rejected and understands the sting. There is no one better to walk us through our healing from the deepest of rejections.

QUESTIONS FOR REFLECTION

1. The best way to heal the wounds of rejection, whether from others or self-inflicted, is to replace them with the acceptance we have in Christ. Do a search for the word acceptance in the Bible and make a list of every verse that stands out to you. Write those verses on post notes, and put them around your house in places you'll see. Say them out loud when you see them.

2. There are lots of stories in the Bible that reveal the dynamics of comparison and its resulting bad fruit. Read Genesis 4, and ask the Lord about Cain and Abel. How do you think comparison might have had a hand in the resulting bad fruit in their relationship? Ask the Holy Spirit if there is anything He wants to show you personally about how that might apply to your life.

-----

1. "When your soul is full, you turn down even the sweetest honey. But when your soul is starving, every bitter thing becomes sweet." Proverbs 27:7, TPT
2. "Nervous System." Wikipedia. Wikimedia Foundation, October 25, 2021. https://en.wikipedia.org/wiki/Nervous_system.
3. See Luke 8:2.
4. See Luke 19:1-10, John 8:1-11, John 4.
5. Song of Songs 2:15, TPT "...Will you catch them and remove them for me? We will do it together."
6. www.bethelsozo.com They have trained teams around the world. So if you aren't able to go in person, they can hopefully connect you with a SOZO trained facilitator near you.

PART III
LIFE'S MARATHON RACE

CHAPTER 13

RUNNING WITH PASSION AND DETERMINATION

"...Then we will be able to run life's marathon race with passion and determination, for the path has been already marked out before us."

— HEBREWS 12:1B, TPT

On a crisp frosty evening in the spring of 1912 the lives of 2,224 people were suddenly confronted with their mortality and the fragility of life. That night the Titanic, the largest ocean liner in service at that time, brushed up against an iceberg.[1] The devastating blow opened six of sixteen compartments to the ocean, and forty-five minutes later, in the early morning of April 15, more than fifteen hundred people perished in the icy waters of the Atlantic. The behemoth vessel, a modern marvel of its time, was thought to be unsinkable.

James Cameron brought this maritime disaster to life in the 1997 film *Titanic*.[2] I was fourteen when I saw it in the theaters for the first time. There were so many fictional characters in the film that fascinated me, but it was the non-fiction storyline of the musicians who played on the deck until the very end that gripped my heart.[3] One passenger said of the brave men, *"Many brave things were done that night, but none were more brave than those done by men playing minute after minute as the ship settled quietly lower and lower in the sea. The music they played served alike as their own immortal requiem and their right to be recalled on the scrolls of undying fame."*[4]

These brothers in Christ laid down their lives as they offered the skills and talents they possessed to release peace into the atmosphere, and they should be remembered and honored for it. Theodore Ronald Bradley—age twenty-four, Roger Marie Bricoux—age twenty, John Frederick Preston Clarke—age twenty-eight, Wallace Hartley—age thirty-three, John Law Hume—age twenty-one, Georges Alexandrea Krins—age twenty-three, Percy Cornelius Taylor—age forty, and John Wesley Woodward—age thirty-two all died that fateful night. It was reported that the last song they played was a popular 19th century Christian hymn "Nearer, My God, to Thee."[5] The familiar lyrics would have been easy to recall to the passengers. All of them are beautiful, but the fifth verse stands out in light of the event:

> "Or if on joyful wing,
> cleaving to the sky,
> Sun, moon, and stars forgot,
> upwards I fly,
> Still all my song shall be,
> nearer my God to Thee,
> Nearer, my God, to Thee,
> nearer to Thee!"

With noble hearts, they serenaded those who were being loaded in lifeboats as well as those hoping for a spot. What a powerful choice they made! Instead of fear and panic, they chose to embrace the power of creative process, knowing it would likely be the last thing they did! What a powerful lesson for every creative and every believer.

AS THE SHIP LOWERS

I believe the hour we are living in can in some ways be compared to those several hours between the iceberg and submersion. When Christ died and rose again, the battle was won. It was the death blow to the kingdom of darkness, but we now live in the tension of waiting for His return and the transition into the next age.

As we sense the lowering of the ship, as it were, will we run for a lifeboat, ready to beg, borrow, and steal to protect our lives? Or, like those heroic musicians, will we simply continue on, being salt and light?

In the shaking, things come into focus. We find ourselves either loving and fighting for our life, or having already laid our life down in Christ. This is the place where our passion and determination to love Him is tested: in the midst of trials.

In Part One of this book, we looked at our identity as image bearers of The Creator and how to recognize His five stages of creative process. In Part Two, we dove into the adventure of catching those sly foxes that try and hinder our ability to partner with The Creator who is also our Bridegroom King calling us to run on the mountains of life with Him. In this last Part of the book we are looking at the bigger picture of life as a marathon. Once we know and believe we are image bearers, and we have said yes to the healing process of becoming His Beloved, then we find ourselves with another challenge—keeping the fire of mature love lit, as we finish well.

Just like in a marriage, after you are several years in, the challenges that affect your relationship are different than those you faced when you were dating or engaged. The focus changes as your love matures. You may not get butterflies every time your spouse of twenty years reaches for your hand, but there is a strength and beauty that is forged through a life that is well-lived together. When we have been walking with the Lord for decades, we have likely moved into a stage of love that requires intentionality and diligence to maintain the fires of love that once came so naturally.

Once we have settled our identity in Christ and done our due diligence to remove the foxes from our vineyard, how do we keep our hearts alive in love while we wait for His return? How do we avoid the pitfalls of auto-pilot Christianity, burn-out, or the "older brother" mentality seen in Luke 15?[6] Thankfully, the scriptures have much to say on this topic. Like the eight musicians who played on the Titanic, we have been given the opportunity to shine bright as the dark gets darker. In order to do that, we must have oil in our lamps, and we must fight to stay awake, connected, and hungry.

STAYING FAITHFUL THROUGH THE NIGHT

In one of the most intense moments in Jesus's life, He spent the night in a garden praying.[7] This wasn't unusual for Jesus. He often sought solitude for prayer, but this was the night He would be arrested, and He knew it. The scriptures are clear that Jesus knew who He was and why He was sent. He knew the cross was coming, and He had already given His yes. Something came upon Him that night, and He was in such agony that He cried out in prayer to the point of sweating drops of blood.

In the dead of night, Jesus was waiting for the fulfillment of why He was born, and he was wrestling with something that was even darker than the night sky he was praying under. His passion and determination to make it to the cross for which He was sent was on display. It's hard for me to imagine the disciples—who walked with Him for years at this point and knew Him intimately—weren't able to stay awake to pray with Him. They loved Him, but when He was in need, in agony, they couldn't keep their eyes open.

It would be easy to judge them from this side of the story, but we won't do that. Instead let's look at some of the reasons they might have fallen asleep and missed their opportunity to serve their distressed Rabbi. When Jesus found Peter, James, and John sleeping, He woke Peter and said this to him: *"Do you lack the strength to stay awake for me for even just an hour? Keep alert and pray that you'll be spared from this time of testing. You should have learned by now that your spirit is eager enough, but your humanity is weak"* (Matthew 26:40-41, TPT).

There was a clear lesson here for Peter. His spirit was strong. This is no surprise. Peter was often the one running ahead of the others, leading the pack, chopping off ears. But his humanity, or other translations say flesh, was weak. I think we can all relate to this. There are times when our bodies just fail us even though our spirit is hungry to keep going. Paul talks about this in Romans 7; we want to do what is good, but we are at war with the sin nature within us that tries to keep us from doing good.

How does this relate to running our race with passion and endurance? Simply put, we need our bodies to carry us to the end so we can fulfill the good works that have been prepared for us in advance—so we can run the *full* course that has been laid out.

Yes, we are spiritual beings that will live forever through Christ. However, right now, our spirit lives in a physical body. If we don't take care of our bodies and manage the modern-day effects of toxicity and stress, we will feel the consequences of those choices at some point. Just ask a marathon runner if the determination to finish the race is enough to overcome a lack of proper training. The answer of course is no. In a sense, taking care of our physical frame can be an act of worship because it is unto the completion of our race, *for His glory*.

That is the literal meaning that I take from the text, but I think there is also a metaphorical interpretation that holds weight. When we grow familiar with those we love, it can be easy to grow complacent, to fall asleep at the wheel, so to speak. In marriage for example, there is a sacred intimacy that happens between a man and woman—spirit, soul, and body. My husband and I often joke about the "marriage-mind-meld" that happens when you start finishing each other's sentences and then even scarier, knowing their thoughts based on body language and breathing patterns.

The danger is, when you are this close to someone, you can start to lose your reverence. You know all their secrets. You've brushed your teeth and gargled mouthwash next to this person. You've shared the most intimate and private moments of life. They've seen you give birth. Seriously, what else is there? But the truth is, they are an image bearer of the Creator. They are a sacred masterpiece and there will always be more that you *don't* know about them than what you *do* know. There is a whole world on the inside of them that you aren't a part of.

Sadly, we don't always treat others with such reverence. Instead, we can tune out, forget to stay curious, and even fall asleep when the other is talking before bed. Staying faithful in marriage isn't just about physical intimacy, it's about the daily choosing to love, honor, and cherish. This destructive familiarity isn't just a danger to our marriages, it is also a real threat to our walk with Christ.

It's possible for us now, while we wait for His return, to grow weary. We can, if we aren't careful, think we know all there is to know because we haven't been surprised by Him in a while or learned something new about Him. The truth is, there will always be more about Him that you *don't* know than what you *do* know. It is imperative that we stay curious, reverent, and in awe of our beautiful Bridegroom King!

STAYING VIGILANT WHILE YOU WAIT

A chapter before the Garden of Gethsemane in Matthew 25, Jesus was sharing parables about His return. He told a story of ten maidens who were waiting for a wedding feast. Here is what He said:

> *"When my coming draws near, heaven's kingdom realm can be compared to ten maidens who took their oil lamps and went outside to meet the*

bridegroom and his bride. Five of them were foolish and ill-prepared, for they took no extra oil for their lamps. Five of them were wise, for they took flasks of olive oil with their lamps. When the bridegroom didn't come when they expected, they all grew drowsy and fell asleep. Then suddenly, in the middle of the night, they were awakened by the shout 'Get up! The bridegroom is here! Come out and have an encounter with him!' So all the girls got up and trimmed their lamps. But the foolish ones were running out of oil, so they said to the five wise ones, 'Share your oil with us, because our lamps are going out!'" 'We can't,' they replied. 'We don't have enough for all of us. You'll have to go and buy some for yourselves!'"While the five girls were out buying oil, the bridegroom appeared. Those who were ready and waiting were escorted inside with him and the wedding party to enjoy the feast. And then the door was locked. Later, the five foolish girls came running up to the door and pleaded, 'Lord, Lord, let us come in!' "But he called back, 'Go away! Do I know you? I can assure you, I don't even know you!' "That is the reason you should always stay awake and be alert, because you don't know the day or the hour when the Bridegroom will appear."

— MATTHEW 25:1-13, TPT

Here again, there is a problem of falling asleep. I find it interesting that Jesus is clearly making a distinction between the five that were wise and the five that weren't, but they *all* fell asleep. Weakness doesn't disqualify us, but wisdom mandates that we take our capacity limits into consideration and prepare accordingly. It wasn't falling asleep that made five of them unwise; it was their lack of preparation. They had no oil when the bridegroom appeared.

The oil is what keeps the lamp lit and burning with longevity, and it represents the Holy Spirit. Our *yes* matters and is of great value to the Lord, but without the Holy Spirit, we can't accomplish much. He is the source of our *light*. He is the source of all knowledge and revelation. If we are leaning on our own strength, we are greatly limiting our potential to shine brightly for the duration of our race.

When the unwise maidens realize that they don't have enough they try to go and buy some. What does that mean since the oil represents the Holy Spirit? I believe it is speaking of a relational transaction, not a financial one. When we choose to trade our time, our most valuable asset, to sit at His feet and let Him teach us, we receive much! The evidence that this is a *relational* transaction can be found at the end of the parable when the bridegroom sends the unwise maidens away and says, *"I don't even know you!"*[8]

This preparedness is important for the modern believer. Every day, we draw closer to His return, and everyday the temptation to fall asleep increases. There is a fine line between vigilance and hyper-vigilance. It's important that we don't become so vigilant that we focus more on the "signs of the times" rather than Jesus. You can tell the difference by the fruit it produces. Focusing on Jesus and keeping your heart alive in love will produce hope and joyful anticipation.

STAYING HUMBLE AND AUTHENTIC

Focusing on Jesus and maintaining a vulnerable and authentic connection with Him is everything. It will protect us from familiarity and foolish choices and so many of the schemes of the enemy. It can also keep us from the snare of what I like to call the *elder brother syndrome*.[9]

This is the heart posture of the older brother in the parable of the Prodigal Son in Luke 15:11-32. If you're not familiar with the story, give it a read. The older brother displays a nasty mix of the spirit of religion, jealousy, and bitterness.

This parable is often taught as a cautionary tale with the wild younger brother in the spotlight, but it shows us more than that. It shows us that we are at war with our flesh whether we remain faithful in the house of the Father, or run off to exotic places in open rebellion. It also shows us the heart of the Father, who is the real hero of this story, is tender and merciful no matter the state of sinfulness we find ourselves in. He received his younger son, whom he thought lost, with open arms and celebration. Likewise, he didn't shun or disdain his elder son when he lashed out in bitter vitriol. Instead, he kindly and mercifully reminded him, *"My son, you are always with me by my side. Everything I have is yours to enjoy"* (Luke 15:31, TPT). How often do we forget to enjoy the salvation that we've received and the kingdom that's been joyously given to us?[10]

Choosing to enjoy your salvation is a matter of perspective and the practice of remembrance. We all have a story of what life was like before Jesus. Some seem more dramatic than others, but the truth is we were *all* translated from the kingdom of darkness to the kingdom of Jesus.[11] What is more dramatic than that? I love the way The Passion Translation says it: *"He has rescued us completely from the tyrannical rule of darkness and has translated us into the kingdom realm of his beloved Son. For in the Son all our sins are canceled and we have the release of redemption through his very blood"* (Colossians 1:13, TPT). Keeping this humbling reality in sight is a powerful tool for keeping the fire of your heart burning steady and bright.

Another glaring lesson we can take from the elder brother is the temptation to slowly make room for more socially acceptable sin like judgment, jealousy, and self-righteousness.[12] This is the hypocrisy of the pharisees that Jesus warned His disciples about.[13] Jesus calls it leaven, another word for yeast, giving us an image of something *we can't see on the outside* that has secretly worked its way throughout the dough. When the dough is then put in the fire *(or testing)* the result is puffed up bread with pockets of hot air inside. It appears bigger and, in the Pharisees case, more important than it actually is. I don't know about you, but that is *not* the assessment I want Jesus to have of me! So how do we stay in agreement with God?

Humility is agreement with God, and it is vital for our spiritual health. Often, when we first come into the Kingdom, the struggle is to understand our great worth to Christ as we fight through our insecurities. It can be unfathomable how treasured and deeply loved we are to Him.

Once this reality settles into our heart, the perfect love of God transforms us, making us an entirely new creation in Christ.[14] The fight then becomes avoiding the temptation to puff up.

We must stay engaged in this battle against the flesh that continually seeks to resurrect itself. Staying in the house of the Lord isn't enough. Membership and regular attendance at church isn't enough to keep your heart alive in love. Just like "staying married" isn't the same thing as having a healthy, loving marriage. Faithfulness is important, but is your heart alive and tender? Are you giving and receiving love freely? Does the voice of your bridegroom move you?

This tenderness of heart is indispensable to a healthy relationship with the Lord. When we first surrender our lives, we are freely given a tender heart in place of a heart of stone.[15] But it is our job to maintain its tenderness. A commitment to living authentically and vulnerably before the Lord is a huge part of the equation. This looks like honest self-awareness, welcoming Holy Spirit's conviction, and quick repentance. An exhortation to this way of living can be found in Christ's letter to Laodicea in Revelation 3.[16]

Jesus says to them, *"For you claim, "I'm rich and getting richer—I don't need thing." Yet you are clueless that you're miserable, poor, blind, barren, and naked! So I counsel you to purchase gold perfected by fire, so that you can be truly rich. Purchase a white garment to cover and clothe your shameful Adam-nakedness. Purchase eye salve to be placed over your eyes so that you can truly see. All those I truly love I unmask and train. So repent and be eager to pursue what is right"* (Revelation 3:17-19, TPT).

Just like in the parable of the maidens we read earlier, this *purchasing* of gold, white garments, and eye salve isn't a *financial* transaction. It is a *relational* exchange. This is made clear by what Jesus says next: *"Behold, I'm standing at the door, knocking. If your heart is open to hear my voice and you open the door within, I will come into you and feast with you, and you will feast with me"* (Revelation 3:20, TPT).

His invitation to repent is received through relationship and feasting. And isn't a feast exactly what the elder brother claims to want from the Father? The issue is never that the Father is preferring another son or daughter over us, but rather, we deny ourselves access to the table when we choose to live in our own strength, forgetting that we are miserable, poor, blind, barren, and naked without Him!

FROM A SPARK TO A WILDFIRE

This kind of authentic living without pretense is uncommon and extremely attractive. When we choose to continually live with our hearts fully exposed on the altar, we have nothing to hide and nothing to lose. This produces a boldness and fierceness that is hard to contain. This is when the spark within us becomes a raging wildfire, changing the landscape wherever we go. This kind of passionate, all-in love is easy to spot, like a wildfire moving down a mountainside. It's the kind of passion people noticed in John the Baptist and went out into the desert to see.[17]

Like a moth to a flame, people were drawn to the radical fire of John the Baptist in the wilderness, even though he was rebuking them and calling out their sins. He openly called out for repentance so that the hearts of those listening would be prepared to receive the Messiah. He was sent ahead to prepare the way for Jesus. The world was unknowingly teetering on a cliff-edge of global transition through Christ, and a sold-out, fiery lover of God was the sign to those who were looking.

Likewise, we are now perched on a similar cliff, awaiting the return of Christ and another global transition. This time the Lord has not ordained one rogue preacher in the wilderness, but an entire John-the-Baptist-generation. We are the ones invited to prepare the way. We are the sign of His return, but only if we are bold enough to love wholeheartedly and abandon everything that hinders love. If we, as a generation, could be bold enough to embrace the fullness of the gospel and maintain the fiery love exchange with Jesus no matter how the world shakes, the world would take notice.

Beloved, you are called into this beautiful honor of preparing the way for our Bridegroom King! As you grow in believing He is who He says He is, and you are who He says you are, you are being made ready to be His messenger. When you are learning His ways and uncovering His creative process in your life, you are being made ready. When you are removing foxes, getting healing and learning to tend to the vineyard of your heart, you are being made ready. When you fight to have clean hands and a pure heart, free from hidden compromise, you are being made ready. When you stay faithful, vigilant, and humble—so that you can run with passion and determination—you are being made ready! Ready to shine brightly through the dark night and ready to run without hindrance the full marathon of life!

So stoke the fire, beloved! Embrace the wonder and passion of first love again, and set your heart to run with fresh passion and determination to cross your finish line in love!

CHAPTER SUMMARY

- Like the eight musicians serenading the passengers of the Titanic, we are called to lay our lives down and use the skills and talents we possess to release the Kingdom until the very end.
- Just like in a marriage, it's detrimental to "coast" in our relationship with Jesus. When we have been walking with Him for a while, our love can grow cold.
- Staying faithful in the midst of a spiritually dark night requires self-awareness and intentionality. Like the disciples in Gethsemane, we must fight to stay awake, stay present, and reject the lie of familiarity.

- In this life, there will always be more about Jesus that we *don't* know than what we *do* know.
- Staying vigilant while we wait for Jesus requires the power and ministry of the Holy Spirit. Like the wise maidens of Matthew 25, we must buy oil in advance by seeking a relationship with Holy Spirit now.
- Staying humble while we serve requires the practice of remembrance lest we forget what we were saved from and become self-righteous.
- Maintaining a tender heart that's honest with Jesus and easily moved by Him should be our daily aim.
- We are a John the Baptist generation that is called to prepare the way for the return of the Lord.
- Just like John, we are called to run with passion and determination that burns brightly before men as we become His messengers.

QUESTIONS FOR REFLECTION

1. On a scale of 1-10, 1 being wet driftwood and 10 being a raging wildfire, where would you rate the fire of love in your heart for Jesus right now? Have you burned brighter or with more intensity in previous seasons? Ask the Holy Spirit for His perspective and write down what you hear.

2. What does your daily pursuit of buying oil look like? Do you have a daily rhythm in place of connecting heart to heart with Holy Spirit?

3. In what ways have jealousy, judgment, or bitterness tried to find a home in you? Is there any leaven trying to work its way into your life? Ask the Holy Spirit to reveal to you any wrong thinking that is keeping your heart out of alignment with His.

4. Read Matthew 11:1-19. In v. 6 of the Passion Translation, Jesus says, *"The blessing of heaven comes upon those who never lose their faith in me—no matter what happens."* John the Baptist was in prison for speaking out against Herod and soon to be beheaded. John knew he was born to prepare the way for the promised Messiah and was wondering if he would see the realization of the promise for which he gave his life. We can infer from Jesus's word of encouragement that his faith was wavering in some way. What parallels can be made as we endure this season of waiting for His return? How can we guard against offense when things don't happen in our timing? Ask Holy Spirit His thoughts, and write down what you hear.

---

1. Wikipedia. 2021. "Sinking of the Titanic." July 31, 2021. https://en.wikipedia.org/wiki/Sinking_of_the_Titanic
2. Wikipedia. 2021. "Titanic (1997 film)." August 7, 2021. https://en.wikipedia.org/wiki/Titanic_(1997_film)
3. Wikipedia. 2021. "Musicians of the Titanic." July 19, 2021. https://en.wikipedia.org/wiki/Musicians_of_the_Titanic
4. Lawrence Beesley, "Last Night on the Titanic: The Musicians," History, April 2, 2020, https://www.historyonthenet.com/last-night-titanic-musicians.
5. Wikipedia. 2021. "Nearer, My God, To Thee." July 23, 2021. https://en.wikipedia.org/wiki/Nearer,_My_God,_to_Thee#Lyrics
6. "The son said, 'Father, listen! How many years have I worked like a slave for you, performing every duty you've asked as a faithful son? And I've never once disobeyed you. But you've never thrown a party for me because of my faithfulness. Never once have you even given me a goat that I could feast on and celebrate with my friends as this son of yours is doing now. Look at him! He comes back after wasting your wealth on prostitutes and reckless living, and here you are throwing a great feast to celebrate—for him!'" Luke 15:29-30 TPT
7. See John 18:1.
8. It's interesting to note that the garden of gethsemane is also called the "the oil press" as seen in The Passion Translation. What better picture do we have of what it looks like to "buy oil" the Jesus receiving from the Father everything He needed to endure the cross before Him.
9. See Luke 15:11-32
10. Luke 12: 32 TPT "So don't ever be afraid, dearest friends! Your loving Father joyously gives you his kingdom with all its promises."
11. See Colossians 1:13
12. See 1 Corinthians 4:5, James 3:13-4:10, Isaiah 64:6 These "socially acceptable sins" are not acceptable to God and the scriptures warn us at great length to guard our hearts against judgment, jealousy, and self-righteousness.

13. See Matthew 16:5-12
14. "Now, if anyone is enfolded into Christ, he has become an entirely new person. All that is related to the old order has vanished. Behold, everything is fresh and new." 2 Corinthians 5:17 TPT
15. See Ezekiel 11:19
16. The footnotes of The Passion Translation for Revelation 3:14 read: "Laodicea means "human rights" or "self righteousness".
17. See Matthew 11:7

CHAPTER 14

RUNNING WITH ENDURANCE
WHILE THE EARTH QUAKES

"We look away from the natural realm and we focus our attention and
expectation onto Jesus who birthed Fatih within us and who leads us forward
into faith's perfection. His example is this: Because his heart was focused on
the joy of knowing that you would be his, he endured the agony of the cross
and conquered its humiliation, and now sits exalted at the right hand of the
throne of God!"

— HEBREWS 12:2, TPT

In order to run the marathon of life and finish well, we need *endurance*. Endurance is the ability to traverse long distances while enduring unpleasant or difficult situations *without giving up*. To be sure, this life will inevitably provide plenty of unpleasant or difficult situations. It's our job to find our way through them without giving up. We should never shy away from the obstacles or seasons of life that challenge us, for those are the places our faith is refined and our character developed. Rooting yourself in a foundation of Truth, maintaining a consistent pace, treasuring your history with the Lord, and living life in view of eternity are some of the keys to supernatural endurance that will carry you to the finish line.

SETTING THE PACE

Obviously, Jesus is our example in all things, and His display of endurance through trials is unparalleled. We will consider His example later in this chapter, but for a moment I'd like to consider His mother, Mary. Right from the beginning, when the angel Gabriel visited her, she knew she would be facing great difficulty. A virgin birth when she is betrothed to Joseph? Obviously, she would have anticipated the dangerous challenges ahead for her on that path. Yet she did not let the difficulty ahead stop her from surrendering her will and life to God's profound invitation. Her calling was to be His mother, and she walked that out with excellence and consistency—all the way to the cross.

I've often wondered how Mary endured the sight of her child suffering such an agonizing death. The heart pain she experienced in that moment must have been soul-crushing. When our children hurt, we hurt. She must have felt as if she was being crucified with Him.

What could have prepared her to endure such a trauma? I believe it was her life of surrender. She was prepared to see her calling as His mother through to the very end, never abandoning Him, by all the little (and big) *yeses* along the way. She and Joseph followed the voice of God step by step as He led them, and after years of walking by faith, they built a history with God. It was this history with God that sustained her through the most horrific event in human history.

She continually said yes to the Lord's leading, *knowing* that her son was the messiah. She had a big picture view of the marathon she was running. She understood on some level, even though Jesus was her son, that He didn't belong to her. She knew their story was much bigger than them.

We see this lived out when Mary and Joseph traveled to Egypt after being warned by an angel in a dream that Jesus was in danger. This was not a small undertaking at the time. They didn't just hop on an airplane and book an airbnb. They chose not to look at the temporary discomfort they would endure but lived with the bigger picture in view—and they didn't give up.

Giving up might be one of the biggest threats to Christians. In my opinion, it's not immorality, bad doctrine, or even the devil that cause many to walk away or cut their race short. It's a lack of endurance. They may start their race strong and think they will always experience the ease and *runner's high* that accompanies any spiritual breakthrough, but when difficulty comes, they abandon their faith.

Jesus told a parable of a farmer who threw some seed. The outcome of the seed's development was dependent on the soil it landed in.

> *"The seeds falling on gravel represents those who initially respond to the word with joy, but soon afterward, when a season of difficulty and harassment of the enemy comes to them, they wither and fall away, for **they have no root in the truth and their faith is temporary**. The seeds that fall into the weeds represent the hearts of those who hear the word of God but their growth is quickly choked off by their own **anxious cares**, the **riches of this world**, and the **fleeting pleasures of this life**. This is why they never become mature and fruitful."*
>
> — LUKE 8:13-14, TPT (EMPHASIS ADDED)

Rooting ourselves in truth is so important. Without this grounding, our faith will be temporary. It might be easy to read this and quickly assume we just need to read the Bible more or gain more knowledge or understanding, but that's not what Jesus said. He said *root* yourself in the truth. This means we must plant ourselves in the Truth[1] and learn to take our sustenance from it.

We must *abide* in the One who *is Truth*. To be like a root means to be like a sponge that absorbs the things around it. When we humble ourselves to receive truth, we are positioning ourselves for the Word of God to find its home in us.

Choosing to root ourselves in truth is an internal choice, but there are external factors that can affect our ability to endure in faith as well. Jesus said that for some, the seed sprouts up and then is quickly choked out by the weeds growing around it—the *anxious cares, riches of this world, and fleeting pleasures of life.*

The thing about weeds is that they grow over time, and it's the roots that do the most damage. They crowd out the other plants by stripping precious nutrients from the soil and stealing potential life from the plant. Maintaining the health and wellbeing of our root system means having healthy boundaries around what we allow to grow in us.

Those are the things to avoid, so what should we embrace? The next verse gives us some insight.

> *"The seed that fell into good, fertile soil represents those lovers of truth who* **hear it deep within their hearts***. They respond by* **clinging to the word,** **keeping it dear** *as they* **endure all things in faith***. This is the seed that will one day bear much fruit in their lives."*
>
> — LUKE 8:15, TPT (EMPHASIS ADDED)

This makes me think of Luke 2:19 (TPT) which says, *"But Mary treasured all these things in her heart and often pondered what they meant."* Mary held the words she received from God through the angel Gabriel dear to her heart. She *clung* to them. This intentionality to treasure His words helped her to *endure all things in faith,* even her son dying on a cross.

The Word says when we do these things we will bear much fruit. Indeed, Mary did bear much fruit in her life. To this day, her choice to surrender, treasure God's words, and endure is an inspiration to us all!

LIVING WITH ETERNAL PERSPECTIVE

It is interesting to me how little we talk or think about death. It is the one certainty in this life that we all share. For the Christian especially, I would think there would be more comfortability with the topic given that our entire belief system hinges on the defeat of death at the cross. But few and far between have I found myself in a comfortable conversation about death.

I guess if death is viewed as an ultimate end, then one could understand the sadness and resistance to the topic, but for believers it isn't the end. Rather, it's a transition into the next part of life, eternal life.

Anyone who has had a near death experience can tell you that facing death changes you. It forces you to acknowledge the impending reality that's always been there and ask the hard questions you likely have about it.

When I was seventeen, I was hit by a car and by all estimations should have died. I had an experience that marked me, and I'd like to share it with you. I think the words I heard in my moment of crisis and the supernatural peace I experienced are simple yet profound keys to help us run our race with endurance.

My friends and I were on our way to the bookstore, cruising down I-75 in Florida. It had been drizzling all day, but despite the wet roads, traffic was still going roughly the speed limit of seventy miles per hour. I was a passenger in one car, and some friends followed in the car behind us. The driver of my car suddenly said in a panic, "They ran off the road!" while looking in the rear view mirror. We pulled off onto the shoulder and drove in reverse towards our friends as quickly as we could with cars zipping past us in the opposite direction at alarming speeds.

By the time we got to our friends who had run off the road, they had escaped the capsized car that lay in the middle of the large, grassy median. Windows were shattered, the frame was crumpled like a tin can, and steam rose into the wet air from the exposed underbelly of the tiny sedan. In a fog of shock, we all stumbled through the motions of checking for injuries. To our surprise, they had all escaped with only minor cuts and bruises.

The unscathed passengers of the overturned vehicle recounted their experience of hanging upside down in the car after it stopped rolling, unhooking their seatbelts, and crawling through the busted windows. What an incredible miracle! Moments later, police arrived who happened to only be an exit away at the site of another car accident.

As my friends were explaining to the officers what had occurred, I walked away and began to pray, and reality began to sink in. While engaged in this time of reflection, I heard one of the officers yell from behind me, "Look out!"

I turned toward the fast moving traffic to see a card hydroplaning in my direction! I turned to run, but my legs felt like tree trunks. I took about two steps and—*bam!* Something slammed into me from behind that felt like an explosion.

I was lifted off my feet, and in that moment as I traveled through the air, it was as if time expanded and slowed down. Somehow my thoughts were clear and stretched with time. I remember thinking, *There's no way that explosion was the hydroplaning car I saw hitting me, right?*

The sliding car had seemed too far away to hit me so quickly. And the sound and explosive impact was not at all what I imagined getting hit by a car would be like. I remember thinking all this, again as time was somehow slowed, and then hitting something a second and then third time. All those thoughts and experiences transpired in a matter of mere milliseconds, but it felt like minutes.

When I hit the ground, I landed under some small bushes, and I knew I had hit my head pretty hard on the ground. One of my friends ran over to me. He was panicking and asking me what he should do. I sputtered out the word *pray*. He looked terrified and said he didn't know how to pray. My body was in so much pain that I couldn't think straight. All that would come to mind was the Lord's prayer, but only the first line. I mumbled it a few times before passing out.

I remember the feeling of passing out—like an old box TV turning off and the screen shrinking to a small circle in the middle of the screen. All the pain went away, and I couldn't really feel my body or it's surroundings. I was standing in a dark room with nothing around me, and I was scared.

Am I dying? I wondered to myself. *Am I paralyzed? Why can't I feel the pain? What if this is it? What if I'm never going to get married. Never going to have kids. Never going to see my mom again?* I began to panic as these deep heart questions rapid-fired through my mind one after another.

Then suddenly, I heard a voice respond to my thoughts. I didn't see anyone, but I heard a voice calmly say, *"No matter what happens, you're going to be okay."* And then peace washed over me.

That peace was familiar. I knew it to be the peace I felt in worship and prayer—the peace I felt when I meditated on the words of Jesus. I instantly understood that whether I were to live or die, I would be okay because even though I didn't see Him, *He was with me.* I knew He had me, and there was no reason to panic or fear death. *I was going to be okay.*

Then just like the TV tunnel that turned off when I passed out, it turned back on. The circle opened back up and—*bam!* I was back in my body, and the pain was excruciating, somehow made worse by the experience of briefly having no pain. It felt like every cell in my body was exploding at the same time, and my mind suddenly focused on a new voice that was yelling loudly in my face. This time it was a paramedic asking me what hurt.

I remember crying while riding in the back of the ambulance. The paramedic was gently patting my arm and just kept saying, "You're going to be okay." Those words were so beautiful to me now—simple words *made new and powerful* because of what I just experienced while passed out.

Through tears, I asked the paramedic his name and told him how much Jesus loved him. In a daze from the head injury and the medicine they were administering, I asked him his name a few times and just kept weeping, telling him how important his life was and how thankful I was for him. Even in such a confused state, I knew that if that was my last moment I had to make it about sharing the love and peace of Jesus I'd just experienced. God had taken all my questions about my future and boiled it down to this one thing: *No matter what, we are going to be okay, because He's got us.*

Since that experience, I have had an easier time living with eternity in view. The supernatural peace I felt was so palpable that it settled the fear of death, and I was able to live with the knowledge that no matter what happens, it's all going to be okay.

Maybe those words seem trite in light of the trials you might be facing. I pray that His heart and peace that I experienced when I heard them will somehow mark you, too. I pray that just the simple action of reading my story will release you into a new freedom to live with eternal perspective.

SHAKING, QUAKING, AND TAKING GROUND

In more ways than one, 2020 felt like that car accident to me. At the beginning of the year, I was cruising along happily, headed to the bookstore, and then everything changed in a moment. For me, it was confusing, disorienting, and frustratingly relentless.

The struggle to try and find the truth in the midst of all the narratives was exhausting and confusing. But God speaks in those dark places, just like the dark room I found myself in while unconscious. And just like the car accident, He brings clarity and alignment to us when we need it most. He can use anything for our good if we are willing to lean in and engage in the process of learning in the midst of crisis.

In the natural, when an earthquake happens, structures that were once safe and a part of our everyday lives have to be assessed and inspected for stability. Professionals have to come and check the foundation, the frame, and all the possible points of weakness that could be potentially housing hairline fractures from the shaking.

Spiritually speaking, I think it is wise to do the same. Of course, Holy Spirit is the inspector in this case, and we would be wise to let Him assess the stability and integrity of our "structures." Are there unanswered questions or places where the spirit of fear has caused hairline fractures in your faith? If you suspect this might be the case, I urge you, beloved, to let Him dress those wounds.

I think we can all agree that the shaking of 2020 was off the charts, and it left a mark. However, the lasting impact on our future and the race ahead of us is up to us. It has the potential to continue causing harm for those who refuse to engage authentically with the questions or pain they experienced. It also has the potential, like any great trial, to produce something amazing.

There is gold in every trial, and if we are willing to dig for it, stay in the process, and let Holy Spirit see us through, the end result will be us stepping forward and taking new ground. Once you've walked through the fire and conquered the thing that tried to take you out, it no longer has power over you.

Jesus is the greatest example of this reality. Hebrews 12:2 (TPT) tells us *"His example is this:Because his heart was focused on the joy of knowing that you would be his, he endured the agony of the cross and conquered its humiliation, and now sits exalted at the right hand of the throne of God!"* He kept His eye on the prize and ran His race all the way to the end, enduring unimaginable humiliation that we will only ever experience a whisper of in comparison. And the result? He took new ground —*ALL THE GROUND!*

Beloved, this is who you've been called to run with. This beautiful Man who is so in love with you that He endured the cross. Let that be personal. Let that inspire you the next time you feel the weakness in your knees and your determination fading. Next time you feel like giving up, meditate on the love of Christ that strengthened and emboldened Him to such a radical act of love. Let the view of eternity, union with Him forever, strengthen your heart and hasten your pace. For He is worthy of your continual *yes*—even through the darkness of night.

Don't be surprised by the shaking. Don't be shocked when darkness tries to kill, steal, and destroy. Jesus made it clear, *"There will be terrible earthquakes and seismic events of epic proportion that result in famines in one place after another. There will be horrible plagues and epidemics, cataclysmic storms on the earth, and astonishing signs and cosmic disturbances in the heavens. ...* **But don't worry. My grace will never desert you or depart from your life. Stand firm with patient endurance and you will find your souls' deliverance"** (Luke 21:11, 18-19, TPT, emphasis added).

In other words, *no matter what happens, it's going to be okay. Don't give up.*

CHAPTER SUMMARY

- In order to run the marathon of life and finish well, you need endurance.
- Mary, the mother of Jesus, showed us what a surrendered life looked like, displaying an endurance that carried her through even the most horrific of tragedies.
- Mary and Joseph demonstrated what it looks like to follow God's voice above all else because they never gave up on the word they received from the Lord.
- Giving up is one of the biggest threats to our faith.
- Endurance is built slowly over time
- Endurance is produced when the word of God dwells deeply in our heart. We must be rooted in the truth for this to happen.

- Endurance is supported when we consistently hold boundaries around our lives that keep the weeds of anxiety, the riches of this world, and fleeting pleasures of this life from stealing the nutrients in the soil of our hearts.
- We must cling to the words and promises from the Lord by treasuring them in our hearts so that we can endure all things in faith.
- Living with an eternal perspective gives us endurance as we look to the prize of union with Jesus forever.
- When everything in our world is shaken, it is wisdom, and unto continued endurance, if we assess and inspect the structures of our lives for damage.

QUESTIONS FOR REFLECTION

1. Read Hebrews 12:1-8. In light of these verses, what is the Holy Spirit highlighting in order to produce and maintain endurance in your walk? In what ways are you prone to stumbling? In what scenarios are you tempted to give up?

2. Take some time and ask the Lord for His perspective on the race you've run this far. Ask Him to show you the places where you could have given up but instead continued on in faith. Ask Him to tell you how that decision impacted His heart. Write down what you hear.

3. Ask Holy Spirit to help you process the last year of your life in particular. Were there any significant events that shook the structures of your life—structures like family, marriage, church, career, government, or belief systems? Ask Him to give you language to ask any hidden questions you've been scared to ask and if He has any questions He wants to ask you. Write down what you hear. If you experienced significant trauma and you think you might need help in processing that, I highly encourage finding a Christian counselor in your area who can walk with you in this season.

-----

1. See John 14:6.

CHAPTER 15

RUNNING WITH LOVE— PREPARED FOR THE WEDDING FEAST

"For now we see but a faint reflection of riddles and mysteries as though reflected in a mirror, but one day we will see face-to-face. My understanding is incomplete now, but one day I will understand everything, just as everything about me has been fully understood. Until then, there are three things that remain: faith, hope, and love—yet love surpasses them all. So above all else, let love be the beautiful prize for which you run."

— I Corinthians 13:12-13, TPT

Beloved, we have traversed some serious theological ground in this book. Hopefully, you have been challenged and comforted and have found Jesus in the midst of our journey together.

We have explored the divine creative process laid out for us in Genesis along with its beautiful implications for our lives. We dove into the transformative process of removing the foxes that hinder our relationship with Jesus. And finally, in the last two chapters we talked about how to continue running the race uniquely designed for you with passion, determination, and endurance. I'm asking you to hang in there with me for one more chapter as we follow the thread that holds it all together from Genesis to Revelation—*love.*

In the end, it all boils down to love.

This may seem like an oversimplification, but truly it cannot be overstated. The Master Artist of Genesis, the Bridegroom King of Song of Songs, and the Father who lays out the path before us as we await His return, *is love.*[1]

Love was the impetus for the creation of everything.[2] Love is what tenderly crafts us into existence, and sustains us now.[3] Love is what empowered Jesus to endure the unthinkable humiliation of the cross.[4] Love is what transforms us as we walk out our salvation with fear and trembling.[5] Love is what carries us through dark caverns of personal tragedy.[6] And in the end, *"there are three things that remain: faith, hope, and love—yet love surpasses them all"* (1 Corinthians 13:13, TPT).

In other words, Love is the reason we *exist,* and the reason we *persist.* We so easily lose sight of this simple yet profound truth and therefore have a stubborn propensity to wander from the goodness of His shelter. Yet, God's perfect love has the power to overshadow all of that nonsense. His relentless, never failing, all-consuming love is like a magnetic field that keeps our souls from wandering too far into our own demise.

We are that one sheep that mindlessly wanders from the flock with our face in the dirt. And He is that good shepherd who leaves the ninety-nine to come and bring us home, over and over again.[7]

No matter what you've been through, beloved, His love is stronger. There's no pit too deep, no heart too sick, and no pain that can withstand the persistent nature of His powerful love.

I love the way the apostle Paul puts it in Romans 8:38-39 (TPT):

> *"So now I live with the confidence that there is nothing in the universe with the power to separate us from God's love. I'm convinced that his love will*

triumph over death, life's troubles, fallen angels, or dark rulers in the heavens.
There is nothing in our present or future circumstances that can weaken his
love. There is no power above us or beneath us—no power that could ever be
found in the universe that can distance us from God's passionate love, which
is lavished upon us through our Lord Jesus, the Anointed One!"

Clearly, this is some really great news, but what makes it even more magnificent is the nature and manner in which He loves. His definition and expression of love is so much better than ours. We often express our love in limited terms and with many spoken and unspoken conditions.

The world espouses a hollowed out version of love in songs and movies that stinks of lust and self-centered gratification. Too often, human love is more of a power struggle or an ideal that is never really experienced but persistently chased after. Because we were made by it, through it, and for it, *we long for it.* But only God's love will ever satisfy. Only God's love can transform us from the inside out and empower us to love Him in return, until the end.

LOVE FREES US FROM THE PRISON OF SHAME

In one of the darkest seasons of my life, I had an encounter with Jesus that changed everything. I was alone in my room praying and organizing a new prayer journal. I had decided that I was going to give myself goals in the areas of Bible reading, prayer, fasting, and scripture memorization. I was labeling the sections of my journal, and I began to weep. I suddenly felt the weakness of my striving and knew that I was trying to earn my way out of the brokenness I felt inside. My tears gave way to groans as I prayed in tongues and allowed the ache of my broken heart to be expressed.[8]

Suddenly I was in a vision, and Jesus stood before me. I was wearing a wedding dress. Jesus was walking toward me, but I couldn't bring myself to look up at Him. My eyes were glued to the floor, flooded with tears. I didn't feel worthy of His love, and I was scared of what I would find if I looked up. My aching heart wanted nothing more than His nearness and comfort to make it right, but I couldn't escape the shame I felt. I could feel Him moving closer to me as my heart beat faster and faster. Then He gently put His hand on my chin and lifted my face to look at Him.

For the briefest moment I saw His eyes, and He said so tenderly, *"Do you think I'm coming back for a bride who can't look me in the eye?"* His passion was pure and fierce, and His words pierced my heart. That one sentence was packed with so much revelation. I understood that His desire was for me to be completely free from everything that hindered me from confidently looking Him in the eye. I understood that He was calling me higher, and I knew it was an invitation to break free specifically from shame.

It was a quick encounter that probably was no more than five minutes, but it marked me. I spent hours pondering His words and journaling my thoughts and prayers to Him in response. I've come to understand that His love for us is completely selfless. He has everything He needs, therefore He doesn't love because it fills a void for Him.

His love is not compulsory, but rather He *chooses us*. He loves not because of anything we have done or will do, but because *that's who He is*. His love is both a rock for us to stand on, offering us stability and sure footing, and a shield around us, offering protection from the onslaught of the enemy. Discovering that it's *this* kind of love He offers gave me a new confidence to believe He could heal my heart and make all the wrong things right.

Psalm 3:3 is often referenced when we speak of God as the "lifter of our heads." Here is how David described this touch of merciful love:

> *"But in the depths of my heart I truly know that you, Yahweh, have become my Shield; You take me and surround me with yourself. Your glory covers me continually. You lift high my head."*

In the footnotes of The Passion Translation for this verse, it reads "In the time of David, to lift up the head signified acquittal when judged, being freed from the prison of shame."[9] That's exactly what I experienced when He lifted my chin.

It has been a long journey of returning again and again to His love to let Him wash away every doubt, but I can say now that even though I am fully aware of my weakness, I am *convinced of* and *defined by* His love. I have the boldness to look Him in the face because I have decided to let His love define me rather than my weakness.[10] That means that every time I stumble I get up and look for His eyes. When I experience uncertainty or shaking, I look for His eyes. His eyes have become my anchor and my compass.

THE ENGAGEMENT SEASON

In this season, between Christ's resurrection and His return, the Bible says we are being made ready like a bride is made ready for her wedding day. Being "made ready" for His return doesn't mean you have to be an eschatological master with an answer for every end-time mystery. When you are about to get married, all you need to know is the heart of the one you are marrying and that your covenant and love will be enough to help you get through anything that comes after the wedding day. Our job right now is to get to know the heart of the Bridegroom King so that we can confidently look Him in the eye on the day of His return.

Regrettably, the modern bride and groom often spend most of the engagement season on planning the wedding. However, a wise couple will use the engagement season to seek counsel. Hopefully, they will learn how to communicate about difficult topics like family, money, and intimacy. A good marriage counselor would encourage them to take time to pray together, dream together, and begin to build a sketch for what their life together will be like. In short, they *should* spend much more time getting to know each other and preparing for the partnership than the wedding day itself. I believe the wise christian should do the same. I have no doubts the wedding feast of His return will be glorious, but we should be more concerned with knowing the One we're in covenant with than the details surrounding that day.

Likewise, the story of your salvation wasn't just the day you were first awakened to His love. That was only the beginning of a life of love with Him. Furthermore, there is an endless number of days we will get to spend in His presence, basking in the glory of His love! Beloved, you are meant to rule and reign with Him forever—*He is looking for a partner to run with, forever.* You are meant to exist within the creative process of relationship with Him, *forever.*

This is your invitation to make yourself ready for that high calling. In the end, the culmination of this masterpiece is a divine duet. Making ourselves ready means aligning with Holy Spirit so perfectly that our hearts cry out in unison!

> *""Come," says the Holy Spirit and the Bride in divine duet. Let everyone who hears this duet join them in saying, "Come." Let everyone gripped with spiritual thirst say, "Come." And let everyone who craves the gift of living water come and drink it freely. "It is my gift to you! Come.""*
>
> — REVELATION 22:17, TPT

Do you have a vision for what relationship will look like with Jesus after this engagement season? Are you compatible with Him? Have you taken the time to get to know His heart? Or have you mostly focused on what He can do for you?

Get clear about what the finish line looks like and, more specifically, *who* you are running with. We may not know the dates and times, but we know that in the end the culmination of creation is a wedding feast[11] and only those who truly know Him will be present.[12] It is wisdom to think of your life now as the engagement season in which you are getting to know your Bridegroom. For one day, you will stand before Him, and your eyes will tell the story.

WAKE UP, YOU LIVING GATEWAYS

In my years of painting in worship, I've experienced the profound reality of being a gateway for His presence and voice, transferring it onto the canvas. Time and time again, I have seen Him move in mysterious and powerful ways through a tube of paint and a surrendered heart. I am still stunned when someone approaches me at my easel after service weeping and testifying of what they experienced while watching me paint.

Is this because I am just a super talented anointed person that gets a gold star from Jesus? Nope. It's just because I've given my yes and then gotten out of the way so He can come through. He can do so much with a willing vessel and surrendered heart.

> *"So wake up, you living gateways! Lift up your heads, you doorways of eternity! Welcome the King of Glory, for he is about to come through you. You ask, "Who is this King of Glory? Yahweh, armed and ready for battle, Yahweh, invincible in every way!"*
>
> — PSALM 24:7-8, TPT

He wants to come through you and be the King of Glory in your life, beloved. Even more, He wants the Bride collectively to surrender so that He might come through us all until His Kingdom is fully manifested in the earth! Can you imagine the glory of the Lord that would be released if the church fully surrendered to her call to be a living gateway? To see this reality in the earth, we must do our part to fully surrender and believe that we *are* who He says we are—*His equally yoked partner and friend!*[13]

Again the footnotes of The Passion Translation for this verse offer some insight. "God's people are identified as living gates and doorways. When God opens the doors of eternity within us, no one is able to shut them. To "lift up" our heads is a figure of speech for a bold confidence that brings rejoicing and hope."[14] When God's people lift up their heads in bold confidence, the King of Glory can come through us. What an incredible honor!

Before we can open up, we have to wake up. We have to wake up to who we are. Most of the church lives clueless to who they really are to the Lord. They may be saved and therefore willing to believe Jesus loved them enough to die for them, but if you ask them how God feels about them personally today, most Christians would struggle to answer confidently.

Our mistakes and weaknesses have defined us for too long. They have held us back from the high calling of being His partner. Our self-imposed limitations aren't just holding us back from running; they are holding back the reward of His suffering.

From the first and second Parts of this book, I hope you caught the invitation to discover God's creative process in your life and to invite Him into every part of your vineyard where foxes might be dwelling. Now, this is where I remind you that you aren't just called to maintain your vineyard for the sake of your personal intimacy with Christ. That intimacy and love exchange you share with Him is meant to be shared with a wounded and suffering world, a world that has lost hope in goodness and forgotten the sound of truth. Your love with Jesus is meant to be a beacon shining in the darkness, reminding the world what real love is. The overflow of your love exchange with Jesus is meant to feed those He brings into your life. Beloved, you are both the bride *and* the friend of the Bridegroom!

YOU WERE MADE FOR THIS

By this point, I hope you have caught the spirit of the invitation being extended through this book. You were made by a Master Artist in His glorious image. That image enables you to create like Him and release new things into the earth. He is consistently and relentlessly inviting you to run on the mountains of this life with Him in any number of creative ways.

Because He is the creative Master Artist, there is no formula for what this will look like for your life individually. Discovering that path requires an ongoing, authentic, unwavering honesty with Jesus. Once you begin to discover the path that has already been laid out before you,[15] you will need to diligently tend to the fire of your heart so that your love does not grow cold in the midst of running with Him in the unique ministry that is your life. *All of this is unto the glory of the Lord being made known to you, and through you!*

> *"We can all draw close to him with the veil removed from our faces. And with no veil we all become like mirrors who brightly reflect the glory of the Lord Jesus. We are being transfigured into his very image as we move from one brighter level of glory to another. And this glorious transfiguration comes from the Lord, who is the Spirit."*
>
> — 2 CORINTHIANS 3:18, TPT

It's His *glory* that transforms us, and the result is we experience, enjoy, and release more glory. You might have your doubts about certain parts of this magnificent invitation to run with your Bridegroom King. You might be wondering how much of this is just hyped up christian language perpetuated by a need to describe and define an indescribable mystery. You might have objections to your ability to have great influence or impact in the earth due to any number of reasonable excuses. To all of that, I would simply say, "What do you hear *Him* saying?"

IT'S TIME TO RUN

Sift through the voice of doubt. Push aside the self-protecting judgments. And lay aside every wound that trips you up. Lean in, and ask Him. Ask Him for a fresh vision of what He wants for you.

I'm telling you, I don't have to know you or your story to know that He can use you in ways you would never think, ask, or even imagine.[16] I know because I've experienced it. I know my Jesus, and His love never fails. He will not leave you. He will not forsake you. He will not fall short like others have. He's not surprised or concerned by your weakness. He only wants your heart. For your heart is a fountain of life, and He wants it to flow with the very glory of God!

If any part of this book has stirred you or caused you to wonder if He is inviting you into something new, I want to encourage you right now to take a leap of faith. Just jump. Don't look at the shadows. Don't allow fear to cause you to shrink back. He will catch you.

Even if you take a leap of faith and it was the wrong cliff, He will use it for your good. He is so moved by your faith and your fearless love that He will find a way to redirect you to where you need to be. Again, He's not demanding you have all the answers or get it perfect every time. He just wants your heart. He just wants your yes.

Can you give that to Him again today? Can you take stock of the things that have hindered you and lay them at His feet? He who planted the seed of faith in your heart is faithful to see to its flourishing.

> *"... I'm fully convinced that the One who began this gracious work in you will faithfully continue the process of maturing you until the unveiling of our Lord Jesus Christ!"*
>
> — Philippians 1:6, TPT

He can transform any heart. He can put courage in your heart that you don't possess. He can give you boldness and clarity to proclaim the love of God wherever you go. He can make Himself known to the world through you, *if you will say yes.*

This is where I leave you and pray that you will fully embrace the high call on your life to love the Lord your God with ALL your heart, soul, mind and strength.[17]

My heart echoes Paul's prayer for the Ephesians that...

*"he would unveil within you the unlimited riches of his glory and favor until supernatural strength floods your innermost being with his divine might and explosive power. Then, by constantly using your faith, the life of Christ will be released deep inside you, and **the resting place of his love will become the very source and root of your life**. Then you will be empowered to discover what every holy one experiences—the great magnitude of the astonishing love of Christ in **all** its dimensions. How deeply intimate and far-reaching is his love! How enduring and inclusive it is! Endless love beyond measurement that transcends our understanding—this extravagant love pours into you until you are filled to overflowing with the fullness of God! Never doubt God's mighty power to work in you and accomplish all this. He will achieve infinitely more than your greatest request, your most unbelievable dream, and exceed your wildest imagination! He will outdo them all, for his miraculous power constantly energizes you"*

— EPHESIANS 3:16-20, TPT (EMPHASIS ADDED)

Amen.

QUESTIONS FOR REFLECTION

1. In light of Ephesians 3:20, what is your *"greatest request, most unbelievable dream, and wildest imagination"*? Take some time to let those things come to the surface and write them down. Ask Holy Spirit what He thinks of them, and write what He says.

2. Ask the Holy Spirit to help you define what Love has been to you in the past, and what it means to you today? Using I Corinthians 13 as a guide compare your definition of love to His. Ask Holy Spirit to help you align more fully with His definition of love.

3. Ask Holy Spirit to give you a vision for the day Jesus returns to the earth. Write it out in as much detail as possible and engage all your senses. Consider doing something creative to express the spirit of what He shows you. I encourage you to share what He shows you with someone. The more we engage every part of us, including our imaginations, the more solidified the reality becomes within us.

4. Using the metaphor of being in an engagement season with Jesus, what's one thing you can do to get to know the heart of your Bridegroom better? Ask Holy Spirit to lead you in how you can use this season wisely to know Him deeply. Write down what you hear, and make a plan to accomplish it.

---

1. *"The one who doesn't love has yet to know God, for God is love."* 1 John 4:8 TPT
2. *"You are worthy, our Lord and God,* to receive glory, honor, and power, for you created all things, and for your pleasure they were created and exist." Revelation 4:11 TPT
3. *"For out of him, the sustainer of everything, came everything, and now everything finds fulfillment in him. May all praise and honor be given to him forever! Amen!"* Romans 11:36 TPT
4. *"We look away from the natural realm and we focus our attention and expectation onto Jesus who birthed faith within us and who leads us forward into faith's perfection. His example is this: Because his heart was focused on the joy of knowing that you would be his, he endured the agony of the cross and conquered its humiliation, and now sits exalted at the right hand of the throne of God!"* Hebrews 12:2 TPT
5. *"Now you must continue to make this new life fully manifested as you live in the holy awe of God—which brings you trembling into his presence. God will continually revitalize you, implanting within you the passion to do what pleases him."* Philippians 2:12b-13 TPT
6. *"The Lord is close to all whose hearts are crushed by pain,* and he is always ready to restore the repentant one." Psalm 34:18 TPT
7. *"There once was a shepherd with a hundred lambs, but one of his lambs wandered away and was lost. So the shepherd left the ninety-nine lambs out in the open field and searched in the wilderness for that one lost lamb. He didn't stop until he finally found it. With exuberant joy, he raised it up, placed it on his shoulders, and carried it back with cheerful delight! Returning home, he called all his friends and neighbors together and said, 'Let's have a party! Come and celebrate with me the return of my lost lamb. It wandered away, but I found it and brought it home.'* Luke 15:4-6 TPT
8. *"And in a similar way, the Holy Spirit takes hold of us in our human frailty to empower us in our weakness. For example, at times we don't even know how to pray, or know the best*

things to ask for. But the Holy Spirit rises up within us to super-intercede on our behalf, pleading to God with emotional sighs too deep for words." Romans 8:26 TPT

9. Footnote for Psalm 3:3 TPT

10. 1 John 3:20-21 TPT *"Whenever our hearts make us feel guilty and remind us of our fail- ures, we know that God is much greater and more merciful than our conscience, and he knows everything there is to know about us. My delightfully loved friends, when our hearts don't condemn us, we have a bold freedom to speak face-to-face with God."*

11. See Revelation 19

12. There are many places that point to this in parable form. Some examples are Matthew 25:12, Matthew 25:30, Matthew 25:44-45

13. "Arise, **my** love. Open your heart, **my** darling, deeper still to me. Will you receive me this dark night? There is no one else but you, **my** friend, **my** equal. I need you this night to arise and come be with me. You are **my** pure, loyal dove, a perfect **partner** for me. **My** flawless one, will you arise? For **my** heaviness and tears are more than I can bear. I have spent **my**self for you throughout the dark night." SOS 5:2 TPT

14. This is the footnote from The Passion Translation for Psalm 24:7.

15. See Ephesians 2:10.

16. *"Never doubt God's mighty power to work in you and accomplish all this. He will achieve infinitely more than your greatest request, your most unbelievable dream, and exceed your wildest imagination! He will outdo them all, for his miraculous power constantly energizes you."* Ephesians 3:20 TPT

17. *"Jesus answered him, "Love the Lord your God with every passion of your heart, with all the energy of your being, and with every thought that is within you.' This is the great and supreme commandment. And the second is like it in importance: 'You must love your friend in the same way you love yourself.' Contained within these commandments to love you will find all the meaning of the Law and the Prophets."* Matthew 22: 37-40 TPT

ACKNOWLEDGMENTS

This book took a year to birth and I had so many wonderful souls that were on my birthing team! Thank you Arin, Anneliese and Elliot for cheering me on and helping me make room in our family for this! Thank you to the team at Unlocking Your Book and Messenger Books! Specifically, Jeremiah and Teresa Yancy and Krissy Nelson, all the other amazing writers, and mentors who poured into us this past year, THANK YOU! Thank you to my amazing friends who helped with reading chapters, giving feedback, and encouragement! Jill Shreve, Heather Farrell, Amber Hodgson, Lisa Schuler and Bonnie Rubin—special thank you for your friendship, and constant encouragement. I'm better because of your friendship! Thank you Fergus Scarfe, Renée Evans, Stacey Harris, Josie Lewis, Sara Thurman, Rhodalynn Jetton, and Elisabeth Darnell thank you for reading and giving your endorsements and encouragement!

I would not be the same if it weren't for the women in the Wholehearted and Courageous community who journeyed with me for many of the years leading up to this book. Specifically Rhodalynn Jetton, Melissa Runacres, Ammie Avolio, Hannah Rabiu, Cherie Cobb, Tiffany Kingma, Jess Eason, Andrea Phillips, and every women I've met at retreats and gatherings—you have left your mark on my life, and for that I am forever grateful.

The leadership of Bethel Austin, specifically Joaquin and Renee Evans —thank you for believing in me and letting me build with you! Lynn and Laura Reed, you covered me in a season of brokenness and loved me into wholeness. Thank you for your beautiful example! Shannon Selim and Lynn Cunningham you were a safe place when I needed it most, and forever family. Lorraine, Samia, Jilliene, Genevieve, and Paul I'm so thankful for your prayers when I needed them most.

To my mom Melanie and sister, Hillary: Thank you for loving me from the beginning, and for always being there for me. Alan, you have been such a gift to me and our family. Thank you for loving us and always giving your heart so freely. To my Dad: I have always known you love me and pray for me. I am so grateful for that and for you. Thank you.

Jesus, my bridegroom King, all the thank you's forever would never be enough. You are worthy of every yes. Thank you for loving me so fiercely and drawing me out of every hiding place to run with you. I love you.

ABOUT THE AUTHOR

Genavieve Gilbert is an artist, author, and teacher currently living in Greenville, SC. Inspired by the Creator and His glorious creation, she paints, writes, and teaches from the overflow of her relationship with Him. In all things, she seeks to facilitate connections between the Creator and His children so that Jesus gets His full reward. She is a wife and mother and spends the majority of her time in the creative process of homeschooling her two beautiful children. Her art has been collected by hundreds across America and internationally. She had the honor of starting and leading the prophetic art team at Bethel Austin. This is her first full-length published book.